Learn To Play The

UKULELE

2ND EDITION

Learn to Play the
UKULELE

2nd Edition

A SIMPLE AND FUN GUIDE FOR BEGINNERS

BILL PLANT AND TRISHA SCOTT

FOX CHAPEL
PUBLISHING

ISBN 978-1-56523-972-2

Library of Congress Cataloging-in-Publication Data

Names: Plant, Bill, author. | Scott, Trisha, author.
Title: Learn to play the ukulele / Bill Plant and Trisha Scott.
Description: 2nd edition. | Mount Joy, PA : Fox Chapel Publishing, [2018] |
    Includes index.
Identifiers: LCCN 2018030366 | ISBN 9781565239722 (pbk.)
Subjects: LCSH: Ukulele--Methods--Self-instruction.
Classification: LCC MT645.8 .P53 2018 | DDC 787.8/9193--dc23
LC record available at https://lccn.loc.gov/2018030366

To learn more about the other great books from Fox Chapel Publishing, or to find a retailer near you, call toll-free 800-457-9112 or visit us at www.FoxChapelPublishing.com.

We are always looking for talented authors. To submit an idea, please send a brief inquiry to acquisitions@foxchapelpublishing.com.

Printed in Singapore
First printing

CD instrumentalists: Bill Plant, Trisha Scott, and Luke R. Davies
CD vocalists: Bill Plant, Trisha Scott, and Carmel Carmody (Ukulele Lady)
CD Harmonica: Luke R. Davies
Special thanks to Luke R. Davies and Mike Couch for their assistance with the sound engineering and production for the CD of our tracks.
Thanks to Peter Hurney (Pohaku Ukulele), Chuck Moore, and Gary Zimnicki for the use of the photos on page 14 and 15.
Thanks to Eric Bogle for the use of the song "Aussie BBQ" on page 70.
Thanks to Ian Fisk for the photos appearing on pages 12, 13, and 52.
Pages 10 and 11: Images of sugarcane field, King David Kalakauu, historical newspaper clipping, Ernest Kaai, and Arthur Godfrey courtesy of Wikimedia Commons
The photos on the following pages have been used under the following Creative Commons licenses: 25 (Nicky Mehta [photo by Nick of Chelmsford, Essex] and Jason Mraz [photo by Moses Namkung]) under Attribution 2.0 Generic (CC BY 2.0); 11 and 21 (Tiny Tim [photo by Christina Lynn Johnson]) under Attribution-ShareAlike 2.5 Generic (CC BY-SA 2.5); 31 (Kate Micucci [photo by Kafziel]) under Attribution –ShareAlike 3.0 Unported (CC BY-SA 3.0). To learn more, visit *http:// creativecommons.org/licenses*.
Shutterstock: 316pixel (80); Amineah (7); Anton Lukin (55); Berti123 (10 photo of Palace of Fine Art); ghrzuzudu (18 top); globalmoments (44–45); golubovystock (51); iDEAR Replay (31); Jason Benz Bennee (21 bottom); Jaturong Srilek (9 ukulele); jesterpop (35); jittawit.21 (56–57); Karin Hildebrand Lau (11 photo of Jake Shimabakuro); Kitnha (8–9 map); MikaHolanda (71); Mostovyi Sergii Igorevich (22–23); Olga Visavi (53); PitukTV (36 TV); Ramona Kaulitzki (7 musical notes); Randy Miramontez (28); Rawpixel.com (48, 49); Robert Cravens (75 bottom); SlayStorm (36 ukulele); Solomakha (2–3); Tang Yan Song (4–5, 7 ukulele); ThongPooN (38); Wuttipong Boonleang (66); yakub88 (11 photo of Amanda Palmer).
All other photos by the authors.

TABLE OF CONTENTS

INTRODUCTION

When we wrote the first edition of this book back in 2011, the ukulele revival had just begun and there were beginners galore. We always took a bag of loaner ukuleles along to our workshops and classes. Nowadays, all the participants turn up with their own ukuleles and a pretty good idea of how to play them. They want more from their music and are ready for the next step. If this is you, then you will love the additions to our book.

WHAT'S NEW IN THE 2ND EDITION
- How to change strings
- How to master strumming and fingerpicking
- How to work percussion into your playing
- How to develop your skill at playing by ear; how to play with others
- Advice on how to become an intuitive, performance-friendly player

When you decide to learn how to play the ukulele, you begin your journey as a musician, soon grasping the nuances of the craft while discovering the joy of communicating with other people through song. We cannot describe the feeling music will bring to you, but we can help you reach it by showing you how to play the ukulele. Keep playing—you will find the joy for yourself.

We will show you how to play even if you have no musical experience whatsoever. And, if you can already play the ukulele, in this book you will find many tips to improve your technique and help you become a better musician—especially when it comes to joining other musicians in groups.

Always remember that you are here to learn, and that the learning experience should be stress-free. Relax. Aim to play music with your very first song. Not only will that set a pattern for your practice, it will allow you to enjoy watching your musical ability improve with each practice session. Don't rush to master the book, but instead progress at your own pace and make beautiful music along the way. When you are relaxed and enjoying the music, your progress will be swift indeed.

Within these pages we present different playing techniques so that, with regular practice through this book, you can graduate from beginner to accomplished musician. To help you, we've included a CD with songs chosen for their range of styles,

strumming patterns, playing techniques, and rhythms.

Progress is easy, and taking things at your own pace allows you to put your personal stamp on a song and develop your own unique musical style. You can adapt our advice to fit your own needs as you grow in skill as a musician. When you revisit a chapter, you will quickly see how far you have come in just a few practice sessions. Soon you will be ready to play with other musicians and can look forward to a lifetime of musical enjoyment. That's when the fun really starts!

Our advice is to go slowly, listen to the music you make, and enjoy it from the start. Along the way you will face challenges, experience breakthroughs, occasionally become frustrated, and have moments of pure joy.

—Bill Plant and Trisha Scott

HAWAII

1

GETTING STARTED

MADEIRA

1879

The year it all started for the ukulele
(see the following pages for the whole story)

GET TO KNOW THE "JUMPING FLEA"

1878

The first of thousands of Portuguese immigrants who would arrive over the next few decades. Most of them were from the Azores and the economically struggling island of Madeira, land in Hawaii, where they went to work on sugarcane plantations.

1884

Jose Do Espirito Santo,
GUITAR MAKER
Taro-Patch and Ukulele Guitars
Made of Hawaiian Woods.
REASONABLE PRICES.
130 Fort Street   Opposite Club Stables,
51·tf.

After fulfilling their contracts as workers, Nunes, Dias, and do Santo open their own woodworking shops, out of which they sell machête-type instruments made from Hawaiian koa wood.

1906

The name used to describe the instrument—'ukulele, "Jumping flea"—is by now firmly established upon publication of the book, *The Ukulele, a Hawaiian Guitar and How to Play It*, by Hawaiian ukulele legend Ernest Kaai (1881–1962).

1891

Hawaii's last king, King David Kalakaua (1836–1891), dies after decades of promoting Hawaiian cultural practices such as hula dancing, the luau, and the ukulele.

1915

A Hawaiian delegation plays the ukulele at the Panama Pacific International Exhibition in San Francisco, introducing the instrument to mainstream culture and the millions of people who have come from around the globe. (Pictured is the Palace of Fine Art, the only surviving structure from the exhibition.)

1879

Aboard the *SS Ravenscrag* are Madeiran woodworkers Manuel Nunes, Augusto Dias, and Jose do Espirito Santo as well as their musical instruments, including the small four-string guitar called the *machête*, or the *braguinha*. Upon the ship's landing, passengers celebrate the end of the four-month voyage with music, dazzling the Hawaiians there to greet them.

1968

In his first-ever TV appearance, on *Rowan and Martin's Laugh-In*, Tiny Tim rushes out through the curtains, pulls a ukulele out of a shopping bag, and performs a mashup of "A-Tisket, a-Tasket" and "On the Good Ship Lollipop" to 35 million viewers.

2012

Dresden Dolls cofounder Amanda Palmer releases "Ukulele Anthem" on *Occupy This Album*, two years after releasing her solo album *Amanda Palmer Performs the Popular Hits of Radiohead on Her Magical Ukulele*.

1926

In a short film titled *His Pastimes* that opens for *Don Juan*, the first feature film to have pre-recorded sound, ukulele virtuoso and vaudeville performer Roy Smeck plays the ukulele on screen, lifting the instrument's popularity to new heights and triggering a buying craze; guitar manufacturer C. F. Martin & Co. makes more than 14,000 ukuleles to meet demand.

Today

The ukulele appears more and more in early musical education programs, community events, festivals, and mainstream music as its ease of play and soothing sound continue to attract music makers.

1949

Guitar maker and plastics manufacturer Mario Maccaferri (1900–1993) begins mass-producing his Islander line of ukuleles, which are made not from wood but from Dow's Styron-brand plastic, selling them for $5.95; TV celebrity and on-air uke strummer Arthur Godfrey (1903–1983) promotes the Islander on his shows, and millions are sold.

2005

Jake Shimabakuro's ukulele rendition of George Harrison's "While My Guitar Gently Weeps" goes viral on YouTube, catapulting him and his ukulele to international stardom.

🎸 HOW TO SPELL "UKULELE"

The proper Hawaiian spelling of ukulele is *'ukulele*. The open single quotation mark that appears before the word is called an *'okina*. The 'okina represents a glottal stop—an interruption of the flow of breath in speech (think of when you say "uh-oh"). The placement of the 'okina can change the meaning of a word.

TYPES OF UKULELES

Ukuleles come in different shapes and sizes, producing all kinds of sounds and tones. If you want an upbeat bright sound, you'll want to use a soprano ukulele, but for something more mellow, consider a concert ukulele.

Soprano. This is the smallest ukulele and also the most popular size. Its light, bright tone is well suited to vocals.

Concert. This ukulele's tone is deeper and more mellow than the soprano, and it has a slightly longer neck with wider fret spacing. Those with large fingers will find it easier to play than the smaller soprano. It also sounds good with vocals.

Tenor. The second-largest ukulele, the tenor is loud and needs to be played softly as an accompaniment.

Baritone. The largest type of ukulele, the baritone has a deep sound that makes it a wonderful addition to a group of ukuleles.

PARTS OF THE UKULELE

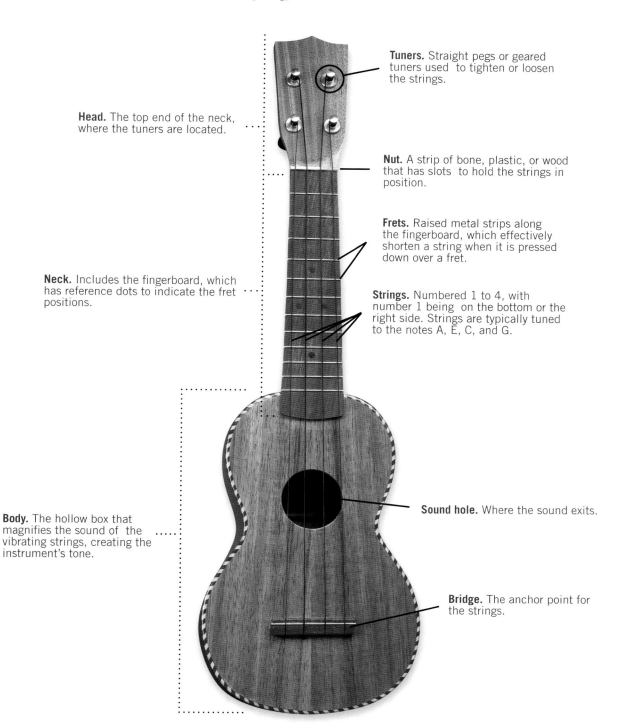

Tuners. Straight pegs or geared tuners used to tighten or loosen the strings.

Head. The top end of the neck, where the tuners are located.

Nut. A strip of bone, plastic, or wood that has slots to hold the strings in position.

Frets. Raised metal strips along the fingerboard, which effectively shorten a string when it is pressed down over a fret.

Neck. Includes the fingerboard, which has reference dots to indicate the fret positions.

Strings. Numbered 1 to 4, with number 1 being on the bottom or the right side. Strings are typically tuned to the notes A, E, C, and G.

Sound hole. Where the sound exits.

Body. The hollow box that magnifies the sound of the vibrating strings, creating the instrument's tone.

Bridge. The anchor point for the strings.

BUYING A UKULELE

There is a wide range of ukuleles on the market, made from solid wood, laminated wood, fiberboard, plastic, or a combination of these materials. Prices can range from a few dollars to many thousands, but cost does not always indicate quality and tone.

If you are buying your first ukulele, take an experienced player along to help you choose. Look for a music store with a range of ukuleles tuned and ready to play. If you go to a store where the ukuleles are still in boxes or un-tuned, the staff might not be as knowledgeable about the instrument and will not be able to guide you in your selection.

Concert ukulele with koa body, ebony fret board, peghead veneer, rosewood bridge, and friction peg tuners by Gary Zimnicki.

Cutaway tenor ukulele made of blond koa with bamboo, gold mother of pearl, and bloodwood inlay by Chuck Moore.

Take your time and listen to as many instruments as possible. You will find a marked variation in the quality of sound between ukuleles, even between those of the same brand and model. A solid wood instrument will actually improve and become mellower with age and use. Keep this in mind when you are considering your options. Most inexpensive ukuleles come with poor quality strings and will benefit from a set of synthetic nylon strings like Aquila Nylgut or Worth. (When you replace the strings, change one at a time so you can copy the original knot sequence.)

Purchase the best instrument you can afford with the best tone and best action. (Action refers to the distance between the strings and the frets; a well-constructed instrument is easy on the fingers and a delight to play.) A local music store is probably the best place to begin. Avoid online sales of second-hand ukuleles unless you can try the instrument first, and keep in mind that a serious musician rarely sells a good instrument.

CUSTOM UKULELES

When you begin playing, it is probably best to buy a ukulele from a local music store. Then, when you find that you really enjoy playing (and we know you will), consider investing in a higher-quality instrument, possibly even one that is custom-made. There are instrument-makers all over the world who are dedicated to producing beautiful, one-of-a-kind ukuleles that are beautiful to look at and beautiful to hear. See page 77 for a list of some of our favorite makers.

Concert ukulele made of koa, maple, and rosewood by Peter Hurney, Pohaku Ukulele.

HOW TO HOLD YOUR UKULELE

Hold the body of the ukulele against you with your right forearm, using your left hand to support the neck. Place your hand near the head, with your thumb behind the neck and your fingers curled loosely over the fingerboard, as if you have a small ball in your hand.

Most beginners grip the neck too tightly and push too hard on the strings. The result is stiff fingers and sore fingertips. As you practice, you will become more comfortable with holding and changing the chord shapes. Soon, you will be able to relax your hand and move more freely around the fingerboard. Then, you can try different positions and experiment with the angle at which you hold the neck.

To get the best sound from a ukulele, strum the strings where the neck meets the body, not over the sound hole.

Some players use a strap around their neck to support the ukulele. Avoid this temptation. Try to get by without a strap, and you will soon be comfortable holding your ukulele on your own. All this may seem a bit difficult at first, but with some practice, it will soon become natural for you.

Use your right arm to cradle the body of the ukulele and your left hand to grasp the neck lightly as coauthor Trisha Plant shows here.

🎸 UKE TIPE: CLEAN YOUR STRINGS FOR BETTER GRIP
Clean your strings occasionally with solvent—denatured ethyl alcohol (we call it methylated spirit or "metho")—to remove the buildup of oils. This will give your strumming fingers more "grip" and result in a brighter sound.

CHANGING STRINGS

Ukulele strings are pretty durable compared with steel wound guitar strings but over time they will wear, start to lose brightness, and become difficult to keep in tune. A good guide to string wear is to run your finger under the string and feel for fret wear indentations in the underside of the string. Many cheap ukuleles are fitted with poor-quality strings that sound dull and need to be changed. Fitting a new set of Aquila Nylgut strings will improve the overall sound of your ukulele.

Unless you need to clean and oil the fingerboard, change your strings one at a time, since this gives you a tuning reference and keeps normal string tension on the neck.

The strings run from the tuners to the nut, down the neck to the bridge saddle, and are attached at the rear of the bridge (see page 13).

Before securing the string at the post end (the head), check that the post ferrule is pushed down flush. Sometimes the wooden peg head will shrink, resulting in loose ferrules. Fix them with super glue. Keeping the string tight, wind it around the post two to four times, pull it through the hole, and wind on tuning tension. Don't cut the loose end of the string until the string has settled into tune.

Once the new strings are on and up to tune, tension each string a few times by lifting it slightly from the fingerboard. This will help tighten the knots, but you will still need to constantly check and tune until your new strings can hold tune.

Many soprano ukuleles have a simple slot housing cut into the rear of the bridge where a knot holds the bridge in place. When replacing a string, copy the knot from the string that you are replacing. Sometimes a larger knot is required to prevent a thin string from slipping through the bridge slot.

The strings on larger ukuleles usually pass over the saddle, secured through holes, then knotted, with the loose ends tucked under the neighboring strings. Before you remove any strings, check the sequence and maybe take a photograph. Pass the new string through the hole, back and under the string, then pass it through the loop. Tuck the tail of the knot under the adjacent string at the back of the bridge.

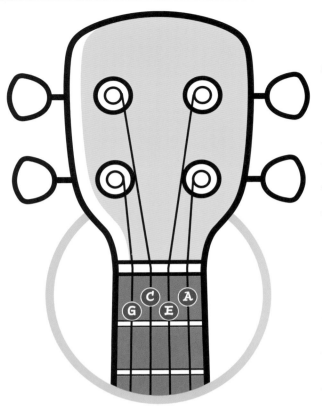

HOW TO TUNE YOUR UKULELE

A new ukulele is hard to keep in tune because the strings continually slacken until the knots and windings take up. You must tune and retune the ukulele until it stays in tune right through a practice session. Get in the habit of retuning before each session, listening to each string as you do so. Be aware that any variation in temperature will cause the strings to change length and go out of tune. Be precise with your tuning, because this will help you develop an ear for the ukulele. Pretty soon, you will be able to tune by ear.

There are many ways to tune a ukulele. All of them work, but for beginners, some are easier than others.

1. ELECTRONIC TUNER

The easiest way for a beginner to tune a ukulele is to use an electronic clip-on tuner that "reads" the vibration directly from the instrument and shows the tuning on a display.

The tuner is clipped to the head of the ukulele so it is not influenced by outside sounds, making it ideal for use in a noisy environment. You can purchase an electronic tuner designed specifically to tune a ukulele, or you can use an electronic chromatic tuner, which can be used to tune any instrument. Electronic tuners have a default frequency of 440 hertz (Hz), so

A clip-on tuner registers an instrument's pitch based on the vibration of the sound waves rather than the sound itself. It's perfect for tuning up in a noisy place.

that all instruments tuned using one will be tuned to the same pitch. The frequency on some tuners can be changed inadvertently, so make sure yours is always set to 440 Hz. Electronic tuners range in price, but you can expect to pay about $20 for one at your local music store.

2. PITCH PIPE

To use the pitch pipe to tune your ukulele, blow into the pipe that corresponds with the string you want to tune. For example, if you are tuning the G string, blow into pipe number four and hum the resulting note out loud. Alternate between humming the note and plucking the string and listen for the difference. If the string sounds too low, tighten it; if it sounds too high, loosen it.

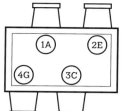

Pitch pipe showing string number and note. These inexpensive tuners (generally $10 or less) have four pipes that are numbered and tuned to the pitch of each string on your instrument.

Some Internet sites and phone apps offer an electronic alternative to the standard pitch pipe, generating tuning tones through your computer or phone's speakers.

3. KEYBOARD

Tuning from a keyboard

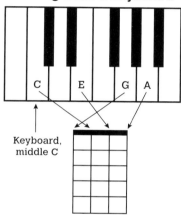

Keyboard, middle C

You can also tune by ear from a keyboard, starting at middle C. Use the same technique that you would to tune with a pitch pipe: play the note, hum it, then tune the string.

4. ANOTHER UKULELE

You can tune ukuleles to each other in the same manner that you tune to a pitch pipe or keyboard. Have someone play a note on one string of the first ukulele. Hum the note and adjust your ukulele string until the notes match. Continue to copy the tuning, string by string. Remember: play the string, hum the note, and adjust the string.

5. TUNING FORK

First tune the A string to the pitch of the tuning fork. Next, hold down the A string at the third fret and tune the C string, adjusting it until its sound matches the fretted A string. Note the C string is an octave lower than the fretted A string and therefore sounds deeper, but it will match. Next, hold down the C string at the fourth fret and tune the E string. Finally, hold the E string down at the third fret and tune the G string to it.

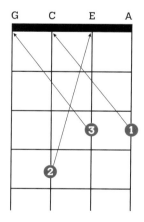

You can tune the A-string of your ukulele to a tuning fork, which costs about $20, and then tune the other strings accordingly.

6. FROM A RECORDING

On Track 1 of our CD, you will hear four notes played on the keyboard in the order A, E, C, G. As each note is played, play the corresponding string on your ukulele and tune accordingly, tightening and loosening the string as needed to match the sound of the keyboard notes.

- Tune the A string of your ukulele to the first note you hear being played on the keyboard.
- Tune the E string to the second note.
- Tune the C string to the third note.
- Tune the G string to the fourth note.

TEST YOUR TUNING: "FRÈRE JACQUES"

Your starting song is the children's tune "Frère Jacques." This song uses just two fingers: the third finger of your left hand to hold a C major chord shape, and your right index finger to strum a simple downstroke in time to the music. If you think this sounds good, wait until you complete the section on strumming techniques. Then you will sound sensational!

Start Track 2 and play along. Tap your foot to keep time, and do your best. Here are the lyrics so you can sing along when you're comfortable.

C MAJOR

Frère Jacques, Frère Jacques,
  Dormez vous? Dormez vous?
Sonnez les matines; sonnez les matines,
  Din din don, Din din don.

Are you sleeping, are you sleeping?
  Brother John, Brother John
Morning bells are ringing, morning bells are ringing,
  Ding ding dong, ding ding dong.

UKE LEGENDS

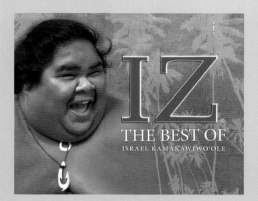

Israel Kamakawiwo'ole

When Israel Kamakawiwo'ole's second album, *Facing Future*, was released in 1993, it became the first certified platinum album coming from the state of Hawaii. While "Iz" (1959–1997) stood over six feet tall and weighed almost 700 pounds, he was known for his gentle manners and melodic voice. He is famous for his epic mashup of "Somewhere Over the Rainbow" and Louis Armstrong's classic "What a Wonderful World."

Tiny Tim

Born Herbert Khaury in New York City, Tiny Tim (1935-1996) is best known for his ukulele-and-falsetto rendition of "Tip-Toe Thru' the Tulips with Me." After starting out as a novelty act in Greenwich Village clubs in the early 1960s, he appeared in the 1968 counterculture film *You Are What You Eat*, which led to a number of appearances on big shows like *Rowan and Martin's Laugh-In*, *The Tonight Show Starring Johnny Carson*, and *The Ed Sullivan Show* in the late 1960s and early 1970s. His first album, *God Bless Tiny Tim*, sold more than 200,000 copies. Tiny Tim was so invested in his public life that he even got married on TV—in 1969, millions of people watched his and Victoria Budinger's wedding live on *The Tonight Show*!

Jake Shimabukuro plays the Byron Bay Bluesfest, Byron Bay, Australia, in 2017.

Jake Shimabukuro

Maybe today's best-known ukester, Jake Shimabakuro (1976–) thrills audiences from the Sydney Opera House to *Jimmy Kimmel Live!*, and from Bonnaroo to NPR's *Morning Edition*. The native Hawaiian began playing the ukulele at age four under the tutelage of his mother before a 2005 viral video on YouTube made him an international star. Jake's father named him after the titular John Wayne character from the 1971 western *Big Jake*—hence Jake's new song, "Mahalo John Wayne" appearing on his 2018 album *The Greatest Day*.

2

THE BASICS OF PLAYING

DEVELOP A PRACTICE ROUTINE

I once asked a really good ukulele player how much she practiced. She replied, "When I decided to become a good player, I practiced for five hours a day, but not every day." You may not have five hours to spare, but you will find that just fifteen minutes of practice a day will make a remarkable difference to your playing.

A good idea is to set up regular short practice sessions once a day or every other day. New students who try to tackle one or two marathon sessions each week often become discouraged and give up, so take it easy. Play with the instrument and focus on making music right from the start. You will be encouraged by the rewards, which will make learning fun and progress steady.

GET RHYTHM

Listen to a song on the included CD and read the associated teaching comments. As you listen, clap to find the basic rhythm. When you have the rhythm down, hold the ukulele neck loosely with your left hand to mute the stings and pick up the rhythm as a strumming pattern with your right hand—this is percussion strumming.

Always keep to the beat of the song by tapping your foot. (Regular practice with a metronome will improve your timing and ability to play with others.) Get out of your chair when you practice. Stand up, stay loose, and move your body to the music. Practicing this way will help you keep the beat and develop a natural tendency to find the rhythm in each song. Your strumming will soon become natural and effortless.

Whenever you play a song, play along with the melody, either from the recording or by singing. Otherwise, you will develop poor timing and your playing will become stilted.

Put down the music book and listen for the chord changes. There is no quicker way to learn than to train your ear. (See page 46 for more discussion of playing by ear.) In time, you will be able to play the chords simply by singing or "thinking" the melody. Don't get discouraged if you have trouble at first. You have plenty of time to learn the more complex techniques. Enjoy where you are right now. The rest will soon fall into place.

Once you get the feel of a song and can incorporate your own style into the music, you will really start to develop as a ukulele player. As you work through the book step by step, you will become more proficient by increasing your range of chords and strumming skills. Then, bingo! One day you will have found the secret of music and become a fine ukulele player.

It is much better to play at a comfortable speed at which you can change chords, keep time, and enjoy the music rather than race through a song trying to keep up. If you find it difficult to keep up with a song on our CD, listen to it for a while until you learn to sing the melody. Then, play it at your own pace, following the lyrics and chord changes in the book. Your practice sessions will be more enjoyable and your speed will increase naturally.

MODERN UKESTERS

Singer-songwriter Nicky Mehta plays several instruments, including the ukulele, as part of the Canadian all-female folk trio the Wailin' Jennys.

Jason Mraz got his start in San Diego coffeeshops before strumming his uke to superstardom in 2008's "I'm Yours."

Kate Micucci played ukester Stephanie Gooch on *Scrubs*, and combines with guitar player and comedian Riki Lindhome as musical comedy duo Garfunkel and Oates.

Coauthor
Bill Plant
on stage

SINGING PRACTICE

Just do it. No matter how rusty you are or tuneless you think you sound, sing your heart out every chance you get.

By learning the ukulele, you also learn pitch and melody, which are big parts of playing musical instruments and singing. The rest is about practice. Every time you sing, you strengthen your singing muscles. If you keep at it you will improve remarkably.

Whenever possible, stand up when you sing. This opens your chest cavity and allows you to take deep breaths and use your diaphragm to push the air from your lungs. Your diaphragm, not your throat, lends power to your voice. Standing enables you to move around easily, which will definitely improve your delivery (just watch the backup singers in any band). You do not need to take big gulps of air when you sing. Breathe deeply and gently at each break in

the vocals. Imagine that the breath goes all the way down past your belly button.

Relax your throat muscles and sing at a comfortable volume. Don't be tempted to shout, because if you sing too loudly your throat will constrict and choke the sound. You may even do some temporary damage to your throat. To avoid strain, always warm up before a singing session: relax your neck and shoulders, stretch your jaw and face muscles (when no one is watching), practice deep breathing from the diaphragm, and exercise your vocal chords by making a variety of silly sounds up and down the scale (do re mi fa so la ti do, and so on).

Make your singing fun by practicing with songs you enjoy. You'll be amazed at the way you progress and the way your improved singing will also improve your musicality on the ukulele.

KEEPING TIME

One of the keys to playing music well is the ability to find and keep the beat. This might take some time to pick up, as each song has its own individual rhythmic feel and tempo. But, with a little practice, you'll soon be strumming along to the beat of any song and adding your own rhythmic flair.

A piece of music is divided into measures of time called bars, and each bar contains a certain number of beats. Time signatures appear at the beginning of a piece of music written as two numbers stacked one on top of the other.

Music encompasses a great many different time signatures, but for starters, try two of the most basic:

Top #		The top number indicates the number of beats in each bar.
———	=	———
Bottom #		The bottom number indicates which note encompasses a full beat.

4/4 TIME

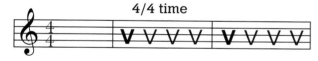

This is the most common time signature, appearing in a piece of music as the figure 4/4 or sometimes as the symbol C, for common time. In 4/4 time, there are four beats per measure, and the quarter note equals one beat.

In the illustration on the left, each V in the measures represents a down strum. When strumming in 4/4 time, you can emphasize the first beat of the bar. That is, play it a little louder so the strum goes like this:

one/two/three/four, **one**/two/three/four, **one**/two/three/four, and so on.

3/4 TIME

Also known as waltz time, 3/4 time indicates that there are three beats in each measure and the quarter note equals one beat. This time signature is played as follows:

one/two/three, **one**/two/three, **one**/two/three, and so on.

Always tap your foot to the beat of the song so that your strumming follows suit. Some songs have rests, or places where there is no strumming at all. Keep tapping your foot to the beat, even through the rests, so when you begin strumming again, you will be able to come in at the correct time and remain on the beat.

STRUMMING

We were at a jam session recently and someone said, "Hey, let's just play songs with the chord progression; C, Am, F, and G." People kept adding songs and the session went on for a very long time. Here are some of the songs we played and a few more as well:

- "Diana"
- "Twist"
- "Young Love, First Love (They Say for Every Boy and Girl)"
- "Why Must I Be a Teenager in Love?"
- "Where Oh Where Can My Baby Be?"
- "The Bristol Stomp"
- "The Duke of Earl"
- "Who Put the Bomp in the Bomp-Shi-Bomp-Shi-Bomp?"

- "All I Have to Do Is Dream"
- "Breaking Up Is Hard to Do"
- "Come Go with Me"
- "Dream Lover"
- "Blue Moon"
- "Earth Angel"
- "Hey Paula"
- "In the Still of the Night"

UKE TIP: LEARN THE MOTOWN MOVES

Watch some Motown hits on YouTube, sing along, copy the dance moves, then play the song while dancing—you may feel silly but your music will be sensational!

What's the point? Here we have dozens of songs all based on the same chord progression. However, there is a huge variation in the sound, tempo, feel, and rhythm across all of the songs. It's all in the presentation. The original bands were lucky; they had different lineups, all sorts of equipment, and professional sound engineering to help express the unique feel and rhythm of their songs. As ukulele players, however, we rely on our strumming technique to give our songs life; your strum is the "make or break" for your song. An old ukulele player once told me that a good strumming technique changes a song from black and white to color. On the other hand, nothing kills a song quicker than the dreaded repetitive "strummania" (see page 50).

When learning a song, it is important to find and explore the rhythm and to express it through your strumming. So how do we find the rhythm in a song? I say, it's simply a matter of becoming a percussionist, then you say "Oh, but I don't have a percussive bone in my body," and go home. But it is really easy to become a percussionist; just start by tapping along with every song that you hear, even those songs that pop into your head from time to time. Tap along to songs on the radio, tap along to TV commercials—anything—just tap along!

For some sensational syncopation, tap along to Latin or African music, or Motown, funk, reggae. To start, choose a song with simple syncopation and listen to where the stress beats are and try to tap out the basic beat. The more you practice, the easier this becomes. Use both hands to drum on your thighs, clap, tap with different parts of your body, move around, and dance. In a short time your skills will improve and you will find that you develop your own riffs that fit very nicely to songs. Above all, you will enjoy yourself. You can also work in pairs, with one person establishing a constant syncopated beat and the other improvising over the top. You can hear this technique at any Djembe drum session. With practice, you will soon be able to identify and respond to the rhythmic feel of a song.

It is an easy matter to shift the percussion work over to your ukulele. No chords yet; hold the strings loosely with your fret hand so that they sound percussive, and with a flexible strumming hand, play percussion. Remember to keep arm movement to a minimum, drop your wrist slightly, and rotate your hand as if to flick water from the fingertips. For extra speed and dexterity you can curl and uncurl your fingers as you strum.

To broaden your scope as a strummer, you can practice a range of simple strum exercises that will form the basis of your strum patterns. Practice them individually until they are established in your finger muscle memory. This may take time, but you will eventually see the point when you start using this technique.

What you are developing is a repertoire of strum skills—not unlike an artist's palette.

The artist combines the colors to create a painting; similarly, you combine your strum components to create a unique strum pattern to suit the song. Because you have established these basic exercises there is no need to think about the process; if you do there is a risk of getting bogged down in the details. Just immerse yourself in the rhythm of the song and relax. You will be surprised at just how good it will sound. As you play with this technique, your strumming hand will develop more combinations. The good ones will be remembered in your subconscious and will reappear just at the right time in later songs.

"An old ukulele player once told me that a good strumming technique changes a song from black and white to color."

SYNCOPATION

Syncopation is a deviation from a regular rhythmic pattern, placing stress on weaker beats or leaving out the stronger beats altogether.

Normal 4/4 time is played with the emphasis on the first beat in a bar, thus **1**–2–3–4/**1**–2–3–4/ and so on. When playing, practice emphasizing either the 2, 3, or 4 beat.

"For superior syncopation and percussive brilliance listen to Peggy Lee's "Fever": https://youtu.be/JGb5IweiYG8."

Step outside the basic tempo and hold back ever so slightly on the timing of a strum; this is a skill that you will develop with the earlier percussion exercises. Notice how it adds to the tension of a song.

19 STRUMMING EXERCISES

1. The basic beginner's stroke is down stroke forefinger, as if you are flicking water off. A

▶ TRACKS 3 & 4

flexible rotating wrist drives this strum with very little arm movement.

2. Down/up, it's a relaxed drag back up with the finger pad so as not to snag any single string.

3. For a bit of swing, vary the frequency and timing of the up and down strokes.

4. Repeated upstroke will build tension and works well if followed by a strong down beat using the V chord up and I chord down (see page 47).

5. Replace a strum by tapping the soundboard.

6. Uncurl your fingers over the strings and mute with your hand.

7. Pull off. As you pick a note, lift your finger from the string almost immediately.

8. Hammer on. Pick the string and then drop your finger onto the fingerboard.

9. Try hammer on the 4th string 2nd fret then strum through an A minor chord (see page 38).

10. Hammer on and pull off a G chord (see page 39) shape, or any bar chords.

11. Slide. Hold the G shape on the first fret; pull out 1, 2, and 3 string while sliding the G shape into its normal two-fret position.

```
A |------0--2---2----0---2---0-
E |---0--0--0---0----0---0--0--
C |-0-------------------------
G |---0-----------------------
```

12. Hold any chord shape and pull out any two or three strings. Here's the opening riff from the Everly Brothers, "Walk Right Back." (See also page 35.)

13. Pluck 1, 2, and 3 strings on G shape, 7th fret; you will be playing a C chord.

14. Air strum (no sound whatsoever)—a very important strum!

15. Upstroke on backbeat. That is strumming on the "and" in 4/4 time like this: 1 **and**, 2 **and**, 3 **and**, 4 **and** . . . Practice; play down stroke on the beat and upstroke on the backbeat with variations.

16. For a bright entry to the strum, strike the G string with your thumb. Incorporate this into any strum combination.

17. You can add a single string pluck on the upstroke. Pluck any strings at first and you will soon find the best combinations to suit your song.

18. Tremolo; strum hand thumb is anchored at the base of the neck, hold the ukulele in an upright position and lightly skate the second finger over the strings.

19. Triplet: fit three strums into two beats. First beat, (uncurl your forefinger over strings, and then continue with thumb down stroke). Second beat, (up stroke). Think: (to-ma)-(to), which will give you the rhythm of the strum.

C MAJOR: THE STRUMMER'S PRACTICE CHORD

Strumming goes hand in hand with playing chords—that is, holding down one or more strings to create different notes. When you work on your strumming technique, use the simple C major chord. When you are ready to start practicing chord changes and progressions, use the information on pages 37–41 and the charts on pages 72–74 to master the chord shapes.

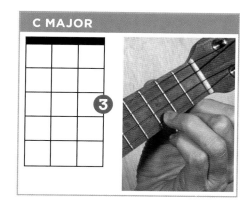

C MAJOR

UKE TIP: STRUMMING BEST PRACTICES

- Keep your arm movement to a minimum.
- Play with a loose wrist and rotate your hand as if to shake water from the fingertips.
- Flex your fingers.
- For a cleaner sound, practice using just your fingertips on your fret hand to fret the strings by imagining a golf ball in your palm.
- DO NOT keep time with your strum hand; tap your foot instead.
- Syncopate your strum; you will not lose time if you are tapping your foot.
- Do not attempt to intellectualize on the placement of basic strum components of your strum. It is enough that you have learned them and that you are playing to the rhythm.
- Keep your focus on the rhythm of the song as though you were a percussionist and the strums you have been practicing will fall into place without any thought on your part.
- Immerse yourself in the emotion of the song. If it is sad, then feel sad, ditto if it is happy, funny, or just plain stupid. What you feel will show, so get into it and enjoy the expression.
- This may seem like a lot of work at first, so take it easy until you start enjoying your percussion sessions. Study your favorite song and find the rhythm that makes it work. Experiment by changing the rhythmic structure of a song to something different from the original.
- Practice one or two strum exercises until they are fixed in your muscle memory and use them while you are learning more.
- Above all, relax and take risks. Focus on the song and the rhythm and not on the process. Let your intuition rule, and those sublime moments of music will be sure to happen.

PLAYING SCALES

Melodies are often based on a sequential eight-note series called a scale. One of the best examples of a scale comes from *The Sound of Music*, when Julie Andrews sings "do, re, mi, fa, so, la, ti, do." The name of the scale indicates the note on which it starts. So a C major scale starts on C and continues upward: C, D, E, F, G, A, B, C.

Scales are the lima beans you have to eat before you can have the dessert of playing a melody. For stringed instruments like the ukulele and guitar, scales and melodies are often written in tablature (tabs), which is a way of writing the fret positions of notes on the fingerboard, so you can play them without needing to read music. See the opposite page for more on tablature

C MAJOR

With few exceptions, a song written in the key of C will be made up of notes from the C scale (C, D, E, F, G, A, B, C). The C scale tablature drawing below right represents the ukulele fret board. The circles with numbers represent the fret positions, with zero (0) being an open string. Your first note you play is the third string open (no fret). The second symbol (2) means you stay on the third string and play the second fret. The next note will be the second string played open, followed by the second string at the first fret, and so on.

The C scale fret board diagram below shows another form of tablature for the C scale. In this diagram, the letters in circles indicate the note you will hear when you place your fingers as shown on the fingerboard. So, begin by playing an open C string, then the C string at the second fret, followed by an open E string, and so on.

G MAJOR AND D MAJOR

The notes in the G major scale are G, A, B, C, D, E, F#, and G. To start the scale, play the second string, holding it on the third fret as the diagram indicates. Next, play the same string, holding it at the fifth fret, and so on. Now, try playing a D major scale using the tablature below.

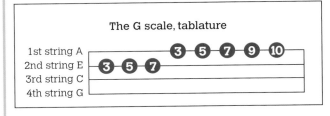

The G scale, tablature

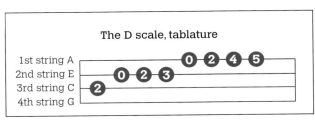

The D scale, tablature

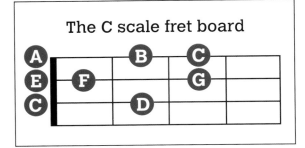

The C scale fret board

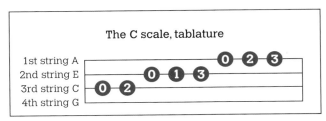

The C scale, tablature

READING TABLATURE

As you've seen from the previous depictions of the C, G, and D scales, tablature is played from left to right, and the lines in a tablature chart represent the individual strings.

Mastering the fingerboard will take time, but if you experiment and listen to your music along the way, you will make good progress; all it takes is time and practice. Be bold and try new techniques. They may be difficult at first, but you will be surprised at how quickly you can learn them. Now that you have an idea of how tablature works, try playing "Twinkle, Twinkle, Little Star" from the tablature here. The song is in 4/4 time.

"TWINKLE, TWINKLE, LITTLE STAR"

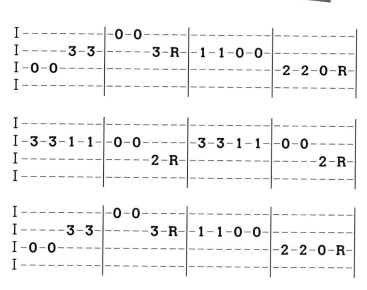

"**R**" indicates a rest for a beat.

"*****" indicates a repeat: play from the first symbol through to the second one, and then repeat the enclosed passage of music.

"AMAZING GRACE"

Amazing Grace is in 3/4 time, or waltz time. We have included the musical notation with the tablature just in case you can find a wind instrumentalist to accompany you (a flute sounds sensational on this song).

The timing is important, so tap your foot and sing the melody to yourself. That will make it easier to find the rests in the song where nothing is played.

Go to *strummania.com.au* for video demonstration.

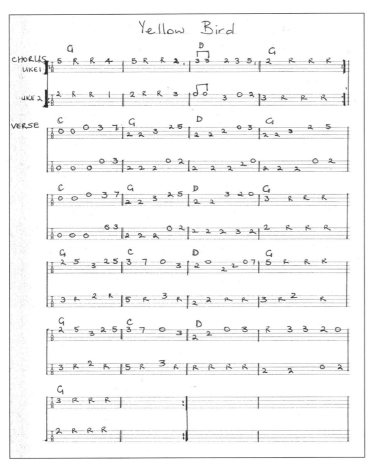

"YELLOW BIRD"

Yellow Bird is in 4/4 time. There are two tab lines, one is the melody, and the other is a harmonic accompaniment. Find a partner and try it. Timing is important in this song as there are periods of rest where it is easy to lose timing. When you play, tap out each bar 1, 2, 3, 4 with your foot and include one tap for each rest (shown as R). You will find it easier to play if you sing or think the song.

Note that the first line of tablature in the chorus has a repeat symbol * at the start and finish. When you see these symbols anywhere in a song, play through to the second symbol then go back and play from the first symbol and then continue on through the song.

Go to *strummania.com.au* for a video demonstration.

RIFFING

Riffs, or lead breaks, are just short melodies, usually played with single notes. If you learn them by rote, they can often sound stilted because your focus tends to be on the riff itself rather than the timing and feel of the song. Better is to learn scales and improvise your own melodies and riffs.

A good example of a riff is the note sequence G–A–B. This sequence can be used to create a transition between a G chord and a C chord. As the tablature shows, you play the second string, third fret, followed by an open first string, then the first string, second fret. Try the sequence again, only beginning it with a G chord and following it with a C chord. A fine example of this riff can be found on the Everly Brothers' recording of "Bye, Bye, Love."

Bye, Bye, Love

▶ TRACK 6

```
A I----0-2-----------
E I--3---------------
C I------------------
G I------------------
```

I've Got Sunshine

```
A I----------0-3----
E I-------0-3-------
C I---0-2----------
G I---------------
```

On the fourth part of Track 6, you will hear the riff from the song "I've Got Sunshine" (performed most memorably by Motown giants The Temptations). Use the tablature to play along—and don't forget to copy the dance moves!

🎸 OUTRO

Try an "outro" to end a song, such as this one for "Crawdad" (page 68). At the end of this slide, play a tremolo in C^7.

```
A I-- slide from 2 up to 3-3-0-------
E I-------------------3-0--
C I----------------------0--
G I----------------------
```

SOLOING WITH PENTATONIC SCALES

The pentatonic (five-note) scale is widely used in all types of music, from rock 'n' roll to classical. It is different from the scales described previously but complements them very well. You can use a pentatonic scale to solo over a chord progression without any clash between the notes of the scale and the chords. For example, you can use a C major pentatonic scale to accompany a C progression of the C, F, and G scales.

To find a pentatonic scale, figure out which notes are numbers 1, 2, 3, 5, 6, and 8 in the 8-note scale. For example, the C pentatonic scale is C, D, E, G, A, and C. Listen to the third part of Track 6 of the CD to hear what a C pentatonic scale sounds like and to play along.

G pentatonic: G, A, B, D, E
A pentatonic: A, B, C, E, F
F pentatonic: F, G, A, C, D

A good way to begin playing riffs is to learn the appropriate pentatonic scale fluently, picking with your thumb and forefinger. Follow the tablature and play the first note with a downstroke of your thumb, the second with an upstroke of your forefinger, and so on. Rest your little finger on the front of the ukulele to steady your hand.

Your progress will be slow at first, but keep practicing until you become adept at playing up and down the scale. Take your time. It takes practice to become proficient. When you're feeling pretty confident, play "My Blue Heaven" (page 67, Track 16), a slow song in the key of C. Play notes from the C pentatonic scale at random over the top of the song. You'll find that some of the notes will be right on the melody, while others will be in harmony. Once you get that down, try playing the C pentatonic scale over some other songs in C.

🎸 UKE TIP: MIMIC JINGLES

A good way to extend your skills while you watch TV is to try and find notes that match the music from shows and the commercials. There are many key changes in TV audio, and playing along will naturally extend your range. For the sake of domestic harmony, though, make sure no one else is trying to watch the television! Eventually you will learn fingering patterns on your fret board that are common to all keys. That's just a bonus; all you need to make music is a basic knowledge of chords.

PLAYING CHORDS

A "chord" is a group of three or more notes played together. The word comes from the Middle English "accord." When you play a song, you play a series of different chords to accompany the melody. To make a chord, look at the chord chart, fret the appropriate string or strings, and strum across all the strings.

To play a C major chord, hold down the A string at the third fret as the diagram shows, changing the A string to a C note. This means when you play you will be strumming a C major chord: G, C, E, C. When you reach the song "Polly Wolly Doodle" (page 60, Track 9), you will see a diagram for the two chords used in the song. Letters embedded in the lyrics, which match the names of the chords, tell you when to change from one chord to the other. This switch from one chord to another is called a "chord change."

First, learn to play your chord changes on the beat as you play a simple strum to a song. Later, as the chord changes become easy (and they will), you can add variations to the basic strumming pattern. Once the variations become automatic, you can work them into your repertoire. Then, simply by varying the strumming pattern, you will be able to create your own style for each song you play.

If you need some inspiration, watch some really good players on YouTube. Remember that each one of them started out by playing a simple strum, and they undoubtedly struggled with chords. Go to *strummania.com.au* for audio/video.

KEYS AND CHORD FAMILIES

The "key" of a song is named after the chord family or scale used to compose the song, and is designated by a letter: C, G, etc. For example, a song in the key of C is composed primarily of notes from the C scale. The key determines the "pitch" of a song, or how high or low it is sung and played. Most songs are played in a key suited to the vocal range of a singer. If you find the pitch of a song too high or too low for your vocal range, you can always change the key.

A basic major chord family in any key consists of three major chords, usually referred to as I, IV, and V. To find the basic chord framework of a key, begin with the key chord (I). Count along the scale to the fourth note, which will form the root of chord IV. Now find the fifth note of the scale, or the root for chord V. These are the main chords you will find in any song.

For the key of C, the chord pattern is C, F, and G or G^7 (C is the first note of the scale, F the fourth, and G the fifth).

🎸 UKE TIP: TRAIN YOUR FINGERS

One of the best ways to learn a chord shape is to train your fingers. First, place your fingers on the fingerboard as if you are about to play a chord. Then, lift your fingers ever so slightly so the strings come off the fingerboard. Put your fingers down on the strings again. Repeat this slowly. Then, without looking, lift your fingers a little higher and hold the chord shape again. This trains your finger muscles to memorize the chord shape, something that will eventually become automatic. The next step is to change from one chord to another until you can do that without looking. Then, practice a three-chord progression.

   Be bold and try to play difficult chords as soon as you need them for a song. With a little practice, you will find them easier to play than you first thought.

DOMINANT SEVENTH CHORDS

The V chord will sometimes include a note that is a minor seventh above the root note of the chord, or, in other words, the minor seventh note of the root-note scale. For example, the minor seventh of a G chord is F and the minor seventh of a C chord is B flat. Including this note gives the chord a slightly dissonant, sad sound. Chords that include the minor seventh note are called "dominant seventh chords" and are written with a 7 after the chord name: G^7, C^7, etc. You might also see them indicated in music as V^7. All the seventh chords in this book are dominant sevenths. However, there are many ways to play a seventh chord, including using a major seventh (major seventh chord) or using a minor third and a minor seventh (minor seventh chord). As you progress, try experimenting with these alternative seventh chords and incorporate them into some songs.

   The I, IV, and V chords form the basic framework for a great many songs. Some songs include extra chords, called "passing chords," added around the melody. There are plenty of great three-chord songs that get along fine without passing chords, though.

KEY OF C

I | IV | V / V⁷
C | F | G / G⁷

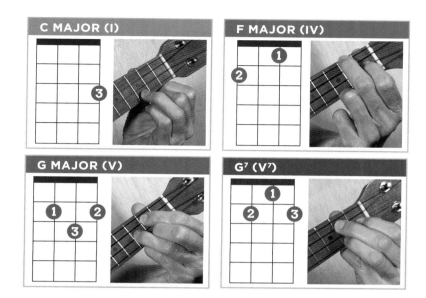

C MAJOR (I)

F MAJOR (IV)

G MAJOR (V)

G⁷ (V⁷)

KEY OF G

I | IV | V / V⁷
G | C | D / D⁷

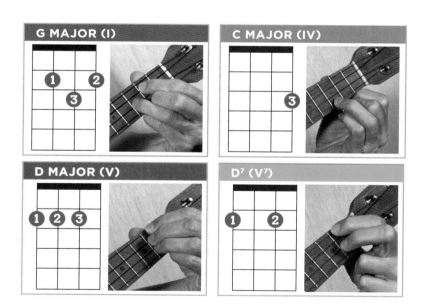

G MAJOR (I)

C MAJOR (IV)

D MAJOR (V)

D⁷ (V⁷)

KEY OF A

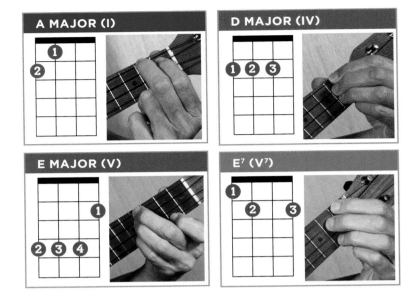

KEY OF F

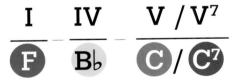

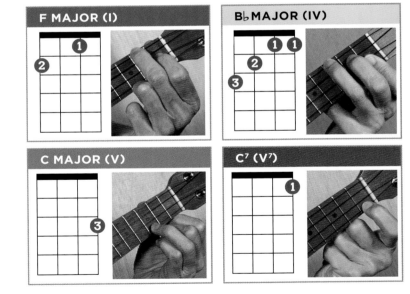

BAR CHORDS

A bar chord is just another way to play the same chord, but with a different sound to give you some variation to work with. Look at the examples below and observe the basic chord shapes under the bar. The G bar chord is actually the F chord moved down two frets with the forefinger acting as a nut. If you move the G bar chord down two frets, it becomes an A chord, and so on.

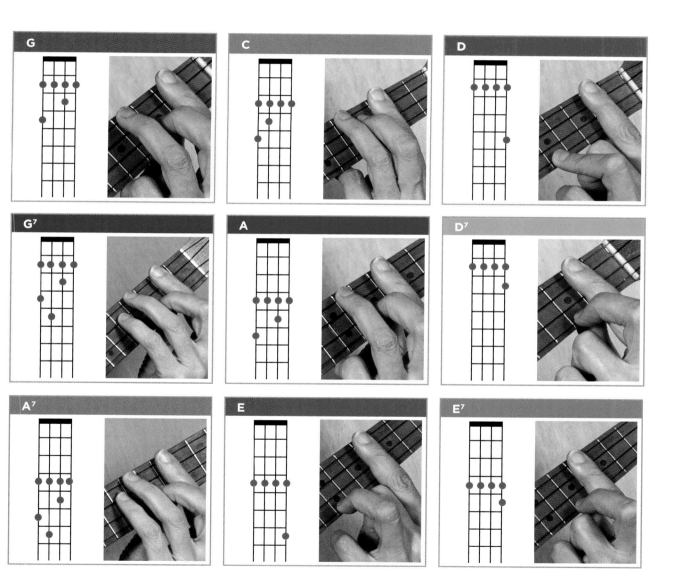

FINGERPICKING

Here are some additional exercises to help you navigate the more difficult fingerpicking songs. We use the following abbreviations: T=thumb, I=index finger, M=middle finger, A=ring finger.

When fingerpicking, it will help if you anchor your little finger to the front of your ukulele, curl your fingers, and pick slightly underneath the individual strings; thumb (T) under the G string, index finger (I) under the C string, middle finger (M) under the E string, and ring finger (A) under the A string.

Try the following exercises. Find video demonstrations at *strummania.com.au.*

EXERCISE 1: C IN 4/4

Playing a C chord in 4/4 time you will be plucking the G string (T), the C string (I), the E string (M), then the A string (A), in that order. Focus on maintaining an even beat for each fingerpick. Play slowly and accurately. Practice until it is stored in the muscle memory of your fingers so that you can play without looking at the strings.

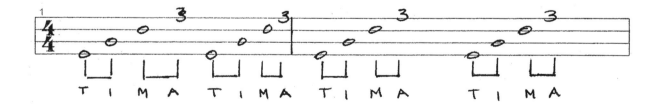

🎸 UKE TIP: FURTHER PRACTICE

Try playing some random picking patterns while playing through the C, F, and G chord shapes. Every string that you pluck will be a note from the chord and will sound good, and some will harmonize with the melody. A good way to learn improvisation is to practice fingerpicking the melody from a song when playing with others.

EXERCISE 2: KEY OF C

Repeat the same pattern except this time in the key of C, fingerpicking continuously as you change the chord shape through C, F, and G.

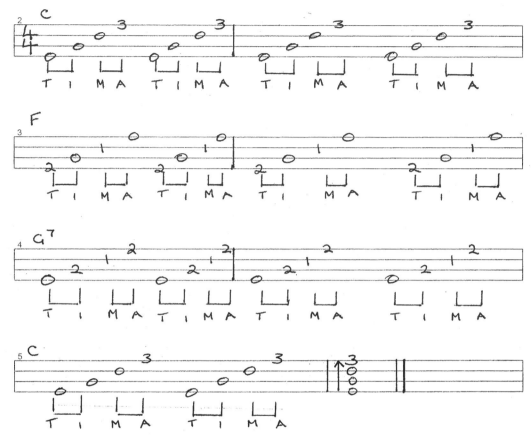

EXERCISE 3: REVERSE ORDER

This exercise is more challenging. Use your thumb and ring finger to pluck the 2 outer strings (G and A) together for the first beat of the bar. On the remaining 3 beats, pluck the strings in the opposite order of the previous exercises (A, C, and G).

As with all music practice, play slowly, and focus on getting the best sound from your ukulele at all times. Speed comes with practice!

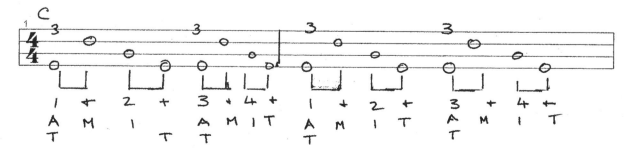

3

Have uke, will jam

PLAYING BY EAR: THE SECRET TO GOOD MUSIC

Nothing liberates your music like playing by ear. When you play by ear, you will automatically listen to the vocals to get an idea of the chord changes. You will listen to your own music. And most importantly you will listen to those playing around you. You will play quietly, sensing and automatically responding to the music, adding your own special contribution. This magical "dialogue" is one of the most exciting things about playing music.

This is completely different from playing with a song chart, which is an intellectual process where the eye and brain take over from the ear. Playing the latter way gives us the confidence to play without listening, and it is this very confidence that so often leads to playing with a loud mechanical strum, which is all too common in ukulele groups. A group of players using songbooks is often a group playing songs at the same time, but not playing music together. Playing by ear, on the other hand, can be much more fun.

So where do we start? We start by looking at the relationship between two or more chords. We do not use the actual chord names because, as you will see later, the same chord has a different function in different keys. To avoid confusion, we use the Nashville numbering system, which assigns a number to a chord in relation to its position in a specific key. Chords are numbered 1, 2, 3, etc., using the root note of the key as the starting point. For example, in the key of C major, the chords C, F, and G are given the numbers I, IV, and V. In the key of G major, the same chords, I, IV, and V will be G, C, and D. By thinking in numbers, we avoid the confusion that results from using chord names.

PRACTICE I–V–I

Using the numbering system, let's look at the relationship between the chords I and V in the key of C (C and G).

Play the C–G–C chord progression over a few times. You will notice that when you play from the C chord to the G chord, there is a feeling of tension; when you return to the C chord, the music relaxes. Play through this exercise until you can

🎸 UKE TIP: FEEL THE PROGRESSION

1. When playing, look out for the key chord (I) and identify with it. Establish this before going on.

2. Get a feel for when the I chord steps out to IV; look for it in your songs.

3. Look for the tension created by the V chord and how it feels when the song returns to the I chord (home chord).

4. When playing in groups, where possible, sit opposite a good player and watch the fingerboard for the chord shapes—every little bit helps.

Learn to Play the Ukulele Have Uke, Will Jam

Almost every rhythm and blues or rock song from the 1950s or 1960s uses the basic I–IV–V chord progression. Therefore, you could almost define rock 'n' roll music as "a small number of chords played to a large number of people," and jazz as "a large number of chords played to a small number of people."

easily identify this relationship. Always think in chord numbers I–V–I. Repeat the exercise, this time with G, D, and G chords. You will notice that the tension is added on the D chord and relaxation on G. Notice that in the two exercises, the same chords have a different function. This is why it is important to think in the numbers I-V-I. When you have established the link between I and V chords, try other keys and see how that works. Now you are ready to look out for that I-V chord relationship in the music you play.

DESCRIBING THE CHORD RELATIONSHIPS

As a ukulele player, the most common chord structure that you will encounter is I, IV, V. In the key of C it is C, F, and G. Sound familiar? We are about to examine the relationship between these three chords. I have heard these relationships described in a number of ways, so it is up to you to find a description that suits your response.

Play through the chords C, F, and G (see page 39) over and over to familiarize yourself with these relationships. You might also try playing the classic tune "Jamaica Farewell"— it has a repetitive I–IV–V structure throughout.

"Think in terms of chord numbers, not names."

Think in terms of chord numbers, not names, and try to pick out the chord changes by the feel of their relationships. Play it several times, but not so much that you will never play it again. You can also practice any song without actually playing it, by imagining the song playing in your head complete with chord changes. Singing a song over and over in your head is also a great way to learn the words.

Be on the lookout for songs that share similar chord progressions. Break each song into parts and practice playing and singing those parts. For example, the opening lines of "By the Rivers of Babylon" are sung to a simple I–V–I progression. If you sing and play it over and over you will start to recognize the I-V-I chord change when it appears in other songs.

I chord	IV chord	V or V^7 chord
This is the chord that often starts and finishes a song or verse and with practice it is quite easy to spot. This chord has been variously described as "home," "coming home," "relaxation," "base," etc. Identifying this I chord in your music is a good starting point for learning how to play by ear.	The IV chord, when it follows the home chord (I), has been called the "stepping out" or "sunshine" chord and can add a feeling of anticipation in a song.	The V chord and the V^7 chord are the tension chords, and you should look for the tension that they add to a song line. This tension often signals a return to the home chord, particularly at the end of a verse or song.

MINOR CHORDS

Minor chords are best described as sad or whining (a child often asks for a junk food treat in a whining minor chord). The best way to recognize a minor chord is to play between the major and the minor chord. Play C major and C minor repeatedly and you will soon spot the similarity between a major and minor chord. Repeat in other keys. Another tip to spot a minor chord is that it often is used in the song where the lyric is a bit sad.

The most commonly used minor chord is VIm, that is the 6th chord played as a minor. This chord is called the relative minor (not to be confused with the banjo player's wife . . .).

THE 7TH CHORD

Seventh chords are a tenser version of the major chord. To get a feel for this chord, play between C and C^7 and then try other major and corresponding seventh chords.

TO SUM UP

Practice to establish a good working knowledge of the relationships between the I, IV, and V chords.

For starters, try to identify the I chord in your songs. Don't look for the other chords at this stage. Try to predict when the progression will change back to the I chord. When you are comfortable with that, gradually extend your awareness to the IV and V or V^7 chord relationships in your songs. Break down songs into simple chord progressions and play them piece by piece. Sing songs in your head and picture the chord changes (it works!).

Of course there are plenty of other chords, but they don't appear very often so don't worry about trying to identify them at this stage.

THE SONGBOOK DEBATE

The debate rages on in our local ukulele group: should we live by the songbook, or should our focus be on learning to play by ear? There is a strong argument in favor of not using songbooks at our public performances because they impede interaction with audiences.

Proponents for the songbook argue that there is a greater diversity of material on tap and of course song charts are necessary when learning a new song or arrangement. Song charts are just that; a chart for navigating through a song, and like all charts they are a reference point only and should be used sparingly. Playing exclusively from a songbook will teach you new songs but there is no doubt that it will also slow your musical development.

The overriding argument against songbooks is their addictive nature. They are so hard to put down that people who have been playing from a songbook for a number of years rarely, if ever, play without one. On the other hand, a large percentage of new players have never played a musical instrument before, and the songbook has been invaluable for their progress. The song chart provides them with everything they need to know—except for the all-important feel of the song.

If we want to take the next step in our music, there comes a time when we must play without following a song chart: just as we learn to type without looking at the keyboard.

Especially when playing with other musicians, the song chart becomes an impediment to listening to what others are doing and also to your own music and its part in the whole. This prevents you from making that special connection that will transform your music.

Moreover, during a performance, a row of music stands presents an actual physical barrier between the players and the audience. Sometimes this is used to overcome stage fright, which is understandable; however, the music stand should be discarded as soon as possible. The important thing in performing is to establish some rapport with your audience, and eye contact is a good start. More about performing on stage to follow . . .

HOW TO AVOID "STRUMMANIA"

In the last ten years or so, there has been a huge increase in the number of people learning the ukulele. For many, the ukulele is their first instrument, and it introduces them to a whole new world of music. Ukulele clubs have sprung up all over the world, ukulele festivals now dot the calendar, and many amateur uke players perform regularly in their communities. There is a lot to be said for the fellowship of ukulele groups and the sheer pleasure gained from singing and playing music with, and for, other people. The ukulele is gaining wider acceptance in the music community and is no longer considered a novelty instrument.

However, the elephant in the room is the standard of play, not the range of songs, which is many and varied. The regular mechanical strum that we call "strummania" can creep in and spoil a good song. Players need to study the feel of a song and avoid keeping time with their strumming hand. As you learn songs and become more proficient with your ukulele, try to reduce your reliance on songbooks. While songbooks are important, continual focus on them will result in you thinking through and planning the next part of the song rather than listening to and feeling the music as it's happening, which is backwards: music is not really an intellectual process but a matter of listening and expressing the feel of a song.

Quite a few ukulele group members have commented on the wide range of playing

"The regular mechanical strum that we call 'strummania' can creep in and spoil a good song."

skills in their group and the need to be more inclusive to keep the better players and encourage newcomers. Better players can be included in basic songs by giving them lead breaks, and better vocalists encouraged to sing harmonies and solos. This will keep them involved with your group and provide the incentive for others to improve.

We urge you to examine your own music for traces of strummania. Work through the sections in this book on strumming and getting the feel of a song. Learn to play by ear and try a little fingerpicking and you will find your music more enjoyable and a little more challenging. If you play in a group, examine the overall playing style. It can be difficult to find someone to give you an honest appraisal of your music; people usually want to be nice and are often reluctant to criticize.

Stand back and listen to how your group sounds (or listen to recordings). If all the songs sound the same, or if this is the comment you are hearing from others, then you have slipped into strummania mode. To get an honest appraisal of your group music, chip in and pay for a professional musician to assess your musicianship. Take notice of what they say and if needed, plan out a program to lift the standard of play. If the majority of the group is happy with the status quo, fair enough, but also provide an opportunity for the more adventurous players to work together with new material. Remember that playing music with others is about music and fellowship.

JAM SESSIONS

A festival or campfire jam session usually involves a group of musicians, who may or not know each other, getting together and playing easy songs. For the most part, the sessions are loosely structured and do not have any hard-and-fast playing rules (bluegrass or Celtic sessions excepted). There is usually a mix of instruments, so it is a great opportunity to join in and play with them with your uke. The best sessions are run without songbooks. You may find this a bit discomforting at first, but persevere and you will soon settle in. It is a great honor to play music with someone that you have never met before, and many good relationships are forged in jam sessions. Sessions played with a songbook, on the other hand, are an altogether different matter and never as much fun.

There is nothing quite as scary for a new player than the thought of joining in a jam session with complete strangers. So here are a few tips that will give you the confidence to make a start.

First and foremost, learn to play by ear (see page 46) to get an idea of how chord relationships work. At the beginning it will be difficult to join in on songs that you are not familiar with, so you need to sit on the outer circle of the group and quietly play along, trying to copy the chord progression, which in most songs will be simple and repetitive. Sometimes someone will introduce a song with an extra chord and often they will explain when and where it is played. If you are not sure of the chords, feel free to ask. People are very generous with their music, as even the best players can remember struggling with chords when they were starting out.

When you are confident enough to join in, sit opposite a good ukulele player so that you can read the chords on the fingerboard and play softly. If you are not sure, don't play at all and just watch the chord shapes and listen until you find the confidence to join in.

🎸 UKE TIP: WHEN LESS UKE IS BETTER UKE

As a beginning player, thrilled with your progress, flush with new chords, and all fired up with the beat, you might often sound like hail beating down on a tin roof. You will find that you usually play enthusiastically and loudly, which can mean that you are playing over others in a group, with no feeling for the song.

You will quickly learn, however, that you will perform some of your best music when you listen and play sparingly. Remember this when you are playing. Stop for a moment and listen. Keep your foot tapping to the beat and try to add a note or two or quietly strum a chord.

When backing a singer, do not play over the top of his or her vocals. Instead, fill a few gaps in between the vocal lines. Do not overdo it. Your time for stardom will come when the rest of the players step back to give you your "break" and allow you to show your stuff.

After a while, you may be asked to play a song. If you are up for it, pull out that two-chord wonder that you have been practicing, take a big breath, and go for it. You will be surprised at how well it will be received; people will remember their first solo songs and honor you for having a go. In the heady rush of success, don't be tempted to sing your second-best song— quit while you're ahead. As you become more confident, remember the golden rule: "Don't hog the jam."

Playing with others in a jam session is one of our favorite things and communication via music transcends words and so often results in music far greater than the sum of its parts. I was a bit tickled to read a scientific paper that concluded that "singing and playing music with others produces endorphins and also improves general health." Well, hello, scientist . . . we all knew that!

That said, for the beginner it can be scary, but take a risk and join in. Remember that there isn't too much difference between the words "terrified" and "terrific."

🎸 UKE TIP: HOW TO START A SONG

1. Tell everyone the name of the song and the chord progression.

2. Sing the song to yourself just to find the right tempo. Start tapping your foot.

3. It is good to play an introduction to show how you play the song and to help find the starting note. A common intro is the last line of a chorus or verse.

4. If you want a big start, then count everyone in with something like "2, 3, and . . ." Or just play your intro.

The best part about learning the ukulele is getting to play with others, as coauthor Trisha Scott is doing here. You will learn a lot by going to jam sessions and festivals.

The kazoo is a wonderful instrument to accompany the ukulele, providing a rich brassy sound. Try using one to play the trumpet riff in Johnny Cash's "Ring of Fire."

GOING ON STAGE

If you belong to a ukulele group, it is likely that one day you will have an opportunity to perform in front of a live audience. That can vary from a low-key community event like a nursing home concert to a festival performance in front of a large audience of ukulele players. Push yourself out of your comfort zone and take the plunge. Who knows, one day you might have your name in lights! Start with the easy gigs, and you will soon be eagerly awaiting your next big performance.

The first thing to remember is that the audience by and large will feel honored by the fact that you are up there playing for them, so that gives you a head start. To give them your very best performance, learn your material well and warm up your vocal chords and your body. A good warm-up will give you a high-energy start at that critical time when the audience gets its first impression of you. A good warm-up will also ensure that you do not damage your vocal chords.

THE WARM-UP

Warm-up exercises work best if the whole band is involved. However, a lot of players consider themselves too grown up for such antics. Don't worry about them. Work out an easy routine and encourage other members of the band to join in. They will soon feel the benefits to them personally and to the overall group performance.

Choose from these exercises but don't overdo it. Start with a gentle program for newcomers and make sure they feel comfortable with the warm-up.

Work out a routine of body stretches, similar to an athlete or dancer's routine.

Follow the stretches with movement such as windmill arms, body rotations, running on the spot, flicking wrists and hands, bending fingers to stretch them, and gently rotating the neck. Stretch up on tiptoes, drop forward, and exhale with a loud sound. Be aware of the physical limitations of the group—you do not want anyone to have a heart attack before the performance gets underway.

Now flex your jaw, tongue, and mouth. Open your mouth wide, move the jaw from side to side, massage in front of the ear around the jaw joint. Move the tongue up and down, round and round, add all kinds of sounds, like "ma ma ma," "me me me," "moo moo moo," and "la la la." Make a siren noise like an emergency vehicle, from a low to high note. Moisten your lips with your tongue and make a "brrrrr" sound like the talking horse Mister Ed (look him up, youngsters). Run up and down the octave without straining. Flex your diaphragm to produce a deep "hut, hut" sound. Introduce these sound exercises gradually to your group.

A good exercise to encourage cohesion in the group is to stand in a circle and have each person make any kind of sound (yell, squeak, hum, yodel, choke, or whatever). Then have the group copy it. If you like, you can combine an extravagant movement that matches the sound. This exercise can be awkward at first for a new group but well worth trying because it relaxes the group and increases energy levels.

Work out a body percussion routine, clapping, stomping, and drumming on different parts of the body. Demonstrate each move and have the group copy it. With everybody circled up, develop a call and response across the circle. Have one or more people clap a solid regular beat, with others adding short staccato riffs. This can be a lot of fun and encourages people to work together rhythmically.

A good exercise is to start the group rocking from foot to foot in 4/4, which is left to right to left to right, left right left right, and so on, putting the emphasis on the first beat of the four-beat bar. This is your starting point and it may take a few sessions to really cement the practice. While maintaining the 4/4 timing with the feet, add clapping riffs and have the group copy you. Later on add clapping riffs that mimic the words of a song. This takes a little practice but it will help the group develop the art of syncopation in their playing technique.

Finish the session with a short relaxation in the standing position breathing slowly in and out, consciously relaxing your whole body on the out breath.

Try adding this sound exercise to the end of the relaxation. Breathe in, and generate a low humming sound from your diaphragm. As you breathe out take the sound up the scale and imagine the sound passing up through your body to your head until it is bathed in the sound. It will feel like the sound is rattling around inside your skull.

WHEN WAITING FOR THE CUE

Keep your relaxed state and avoid the inevitable backstage chatterers that want to make everyone feel as anxious as they feel. Stay focused despite your nervous excitement; a measure of nervous excitement will benefit your performance. Go somewhere quiet and check the tuning of your ukulele. You should know your songs by now, so don't worry about forgetting them on stage, or there is a good chance that you will. If you need a songbook, try to use it as a reference only.

When it is time to step out into the lights, relish the buzz and acknowledge the audience by looking at them. If you find this difficult, scan the back wall just above their heads with a knowing grin that says, "This will be fun." If you want to see similar tricks in action, then watch a politician at an election rally. If you are not comfortable with making eye contact, then scan foreheads of the audience, or keep your mind occupied with their hairstyles. Above all else, smile! When you eventually gain the confidence to make eye contact, you will always find someone who is really enjoying the performance and will acknowledge you with a smile. Smile back at them as if to say, "Yeah, this is fun," and it will be.

We all make mistakes when performing. We play wrong chords, forget words, get croaky; well, at least I do, and often. Just remember that most of the time the audience either doesn't notice or chooses to ignore these little mistakes. Whatever you do, don't freak out and dry up. Soldier on regardless.

Keeping your energy up during a performance requires practice and skill. Watch out for flagging energy in your performance, push yourself to keep your peak, and know when to end the show. You can try a sugar or caffeine hit before you go on, but avoid alcohol . . . it just doesn't work.

Know when to stop a performance. You will learn to recognize the signs. If you are near the end of your gig, stop and take your bow.

Remember, prepare well, warm up, give it your best, and above all enjoy yourself and never forget that you are giving your audience a gift.

And you can feel good about that.

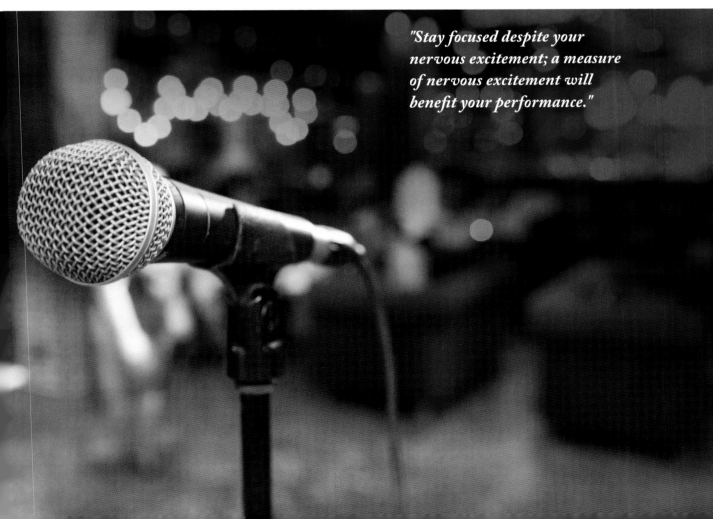

"Stay focused despite your nervous excitement; a measure of nervous excitement will benefit your performance."

4
SONGBOOK

12-BAR BLUES

The 12-bar blues is a standard progression that forms the basis for a multitude of rhythm and blues and rock and roll songs. There are many variations on this basic progression, but the idea remains the same.

In the table below, each box represents one bar of 4/4 time, where the chord number is played on each beat.

The last bar (chord V or V^7) is called the turnaround. It takes the song back to the next 12-bar sequence and so on, until everyone gets sick of playing, and then a I chord is used to finish the song. Of course, there are many variations of this common basic pattern.

Listen to some of your favorite songs and see how many you can find that exactly fit or are derived from the 12-bar blues pattern. Here are some examples:

- "Blue Suede Shoes"
- "Hound Dog"
- "In the Mood"
- "Jailhouse Rock"
- "Johnny B. Goode"
- "Kansas City Blues"
- "Shake, Rattle, and Roll"
- "Sweet Home Chicago"
- "Tutti Frutti"

A 12-bar blues session provides a great opportunity to improvise with bar chords, second and third position chords, and fingerpicking.

If we use the chord numbering system, the 12-bar progression looks like this:

First four bars	I/I/I/I	I/I/I/I	I/I/I/I	$I^7/I^7/I^7/I^7$
Second four bars	IV/IV/IV/IV	IV/IV/IV/IV	I/I/I/I	I/I/I/I
Final four bars	V/V/V/V	IV/IV/IV/IV	I/I/I/I	V/V/V/V

So, in the key of G, the progression is played like this:

First four bars	G/G/G/G	G/G/G/G	G/G/G/G	$G^7/G^7/G^7/G^7$
Second four bars	C/C/C/C	C/C/C/C	G/G/G/G	G/G/G/G
Final four bars	D/D/D/D	C/C/C/C	G/G/G/G	D/D/D/D

"LEARN TO PLAY THE UKULELE OVERNIGHT BLUES" ▶ TRACK 8

Playing the blues is really easy and a lot of fun. Using the chord progression on page 58, follow the recording and play the progression all the way through over and over. As the track progresses, you will hear that we add some words and a few mates will join in with other instruments. You can sing along to this song, which we call "Learn to Play the Ukulele Overnight Blues." Musically it may sound a bit complicated, but the basic progression will remain the same throughout. Keep playing. If you get lost, wait until the next round and start again. You may soon be able to recognize when each line of the progression starts on the CD.

When you listen on the computer, select an easy section and play it for a while in a repeating loop. For the first two lines of each verse, play G–G–G–G⁷. For the third line, play C–C–G–G. For the last line, play D–C–G–D.

If you're sick of the TV, you got nothin' to do,
    Well listen up, baby, we've got something for you,
You can learn the ukulele, you can learn it overnight,
    So open up the book and we'll show you how to do it right,

First you tune up your uke and then you learn how to strum,
    You drive the cat crazy with that Brother John,
And your fingers are hurtin', and your arm is gettin' numb,
    The book has the nerve to tell you that this is all fun!

It's OK for the authors, 'cause they know all the chords,
    But we gotta practice 'til we're totally bored,
Then there's a scale pentatonic, whatever that may be,
    There's even 4/4 time and something called the key of C.

But the songs ain't half bad if you can just strum along,
    There's the midnight special and a sloop called John,
I know I'll learn to play, it won't take me long.
    I'll learn to lose these, learn to play the ukulele . . .
overnight blues.

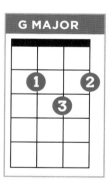

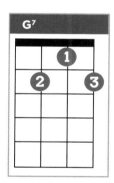

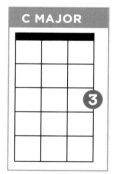

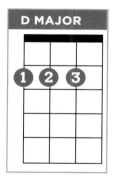

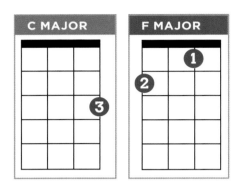

"POLLY WOLLY DOODLE"

For this song, the first verse and chorus are played with a basic down strum in 4/4 time. Strum with the beat and emphasize the first beat of each bar. After that, try a mixture of down and up strums and be more adventurous with your strumming style. Sometimes the chorus incorporates a down up/down strum each time you sing the words "fare thee well." When this happens, play two down strums to complete the bar. For the most part, chord changes occur on the words "day" and "fey." Close the book and play by ear to see if you can pick the chord changes.

4/4

Intro
C–C–C–C, F–Rest–Rest–Rest. (That is, play C for four strums, then F for one strum, and rest for the remaining three beats. Then, begin the first verse.)

First verse
Oh, **F** I went down south for to see my Sal,
   Singing Polly Wolly Doodle all the **C** day,
My Sal, she is a saucy gal,
   Singing Polly Wolly Doodle all the **F** day!

Chorus
F Fare thee well, fare thee well, fare thee well my fairy **C** fey,
   Goin' to Louisiana,
For to see my Susyanna,
   Singing Polly Wolly Doodle all the **F** day!

Second verse
F Behind the barn, down on my knees,
   Singing Polly Wolly Doodle all the **C** day,
I thought I heard a chicken sneeze,
   Singing Polly Wolly Doodle all the **F** day!

Repeat Chorus

Third verse
F Oh, a grasshopper sittin' on a railroad track,
   Singing Polly Wolly Doodle all the **C** day,
Pickin' his teeth with a carpet tack,
   Singing Polly Wolly Doodle all the **F** day!

Repeat Chorus

Fourth verse
F Came to a river and I couldn't get across,
   Singing Polly Wolly Doodle all the **C** day,
I jumped on a gator 'cause I thought it was my hoss,
   Singing Polly Wolly Doodle all the **F** day!

Repeat Chorus

"PAY ME MY MONEY DOWN" ►TRACK 10

Random picking with thumb and fingers suits the upbeat
tempo of this song. There is a strong emphasis on striking the G
string with the thumb, followed by a random pluck on any other
string or strings on the upstroke. There is also an occasional light
down strum on all the strings. At the finish, play an abrupt F
chord. Try using a choke.

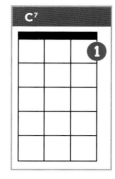
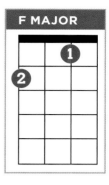

4/4

Intro
C⁷–C⁷–C⁷–C⁷, F–Rest–Rest–Rest

First verse
F Thought I heard the captain say,
    Pay me my **C⁷** money down,
Tomorrow is our sailing day,
    Pay me my **F** money down.

Chorus
F Pay me, pay me,
    Pay me my **C⁷** money down,
Pay me or go to jail,
    Pay me my **F** money down.

Second verse
F The very next day he cleared the bar,
    Pay me my **C⁷** money down,
He knocked me down with the end of a spar,
    Pay me my **F** money down.

Repeat Chorus

Third verse
F Well, I wish I was Mr. Steven's son,
    Pay me my **C⁷** money down,
Sit on the bank and watch the work done,
    Pay me my **F** money down.

Repeat Chorus

Fourth verse
F Wish I was a rich man's son,
    Pay me my **C⁷** money down,
Sit on the bank and watch the river run,
    Pay me my **F** money down.

Final chorus
F Pay me, pay me,
    Pay me my **C⁷** money down,
Pay me or go to jail,
    Pay me my **F** money down.

Instrumental Chorus

F Pay me, pay me,
    Pay me my **C⁷** money down,
Pay me or go to jail,
    Pay me my **F** money down.

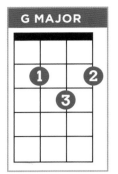

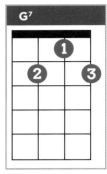

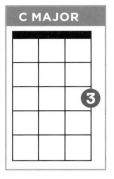

"JAMBALAYA"

Words and music by Hank Williams

To give this song that country feel, try plucking the G string at the start of each bar, followed by a down strum for the second beat; repeat the pluck and strum to complete the bar. For your first try, you might like to substitute a G^7 chord for G.

4/4

Intro

G–G–G–G, G^7–G^7–G^7–G^7, C–C–C–C

First verse

C Good-bye, Joe, me gotta go, me oh **G** my oh,
Me gotta go pole the **G7** pirogue down the **C** bayou,
My Yvonne, the sweetest one, me oh **G** my oh,
Son of a gun, we'll have big **G7** fun on the **C** bayou.

Chorus

C Jambalaya, crawfish pie, filé **G** gumbo,
'Cause tonight I'm gonna **G7** see my ma cher **C** amio,
Pick guitar, fill fruit jar, and be **G** gay-o,
Son of a gun, we'll have big **G7** fun on the **C** bayou.

Second verse

C Thibodaux, Fontaineaux, the place is **G** a-buzzin,'
Kinfolk come to see **G7** Yvonne by the **C** dozen,
Dress in style and go hog wild, me oh **G** my oh,
Son of a gun, we'll have big **G7** fun on the **C** bayou.

Repeat Chorus

Third verse

C Settle down far from town; get me a **G** pirogue,
And I'll catch all the **G7** fish in the **C** bayou,
Swap my mon to buy Yvonne what she **G** need-o,
Son of a gun, we'll have big **G7** fun on the **C** bayou.

Final chorus

C Jambalaya, crawfish pie, filé **G** gumbo,
'Cause tonight I'm gonna **G7** see my ma cher **C** amio.
Pick guitar, fill fruit jar, and be **G** gay-o,
Son of a gun, we'll have big **G7** fun on the **C** bayou,
Son of a **G** gun, we'll have big **G7** fun on the **C** bayou.

► TRACK 12

"THIS TRAIN IS BOUND FOR GLORY"

Of course this number has the "chunka" feel of a train. When you play in a group, you can mute the strings now and again to emphasize the train-like rhythm.

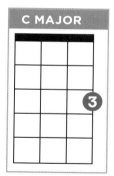

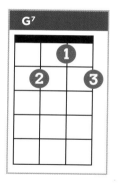

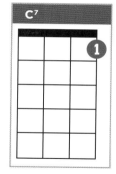

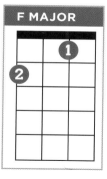

4/4

Intro
C–C–C–C, G^7–G^7–G^7–G^7, C–C–C–C

Chorus
C This train is bound for glory, this train,
This train is bound for glory, **G7** this train,
C This train is **C7** bound for glory,
F Don't ride nothin' but the righteous and the holy,
C This train is **G7** bound for glory, this **C** train.

First verse
C This train don't carry no gamblers, this train,
This train don't carry no gamblers, **G7** this train,
C This train don't **C7** carry no gamblers,
F No hypocrites, no midnight ramblers,
C This train is **G7** bound for glory, this **C** train.

Repeat Chorus

Second verse
C This train is built for speed now, this train,
This train is built for speed now, **G7** this train,
C This train is **C7** built for speed now,
F Fastest train that you ever did see now,
C This train is **G7** bound for glory, **C** this train.

Instrumental Chorus

Third verse
C This train don't carry no rustlers, this train,
C This train don't carry no rustlers, **G7** this train,
C This train don't **C7** carry no rustlers,
F No street walkers, two-bit hustlers,
C This train is **G7** bound for glory, this **C** train.

Repeat Chorus

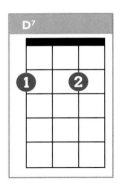

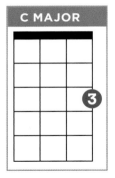

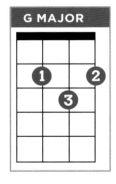

"MIDNIGHT SPECIAL" ▶ TRACK 13
by Huddie Ledbetter

Experiment with this version of the D⁷ chord, sometimes referred to as the Hawaiian D⁷. This slow bluesy version will give you an opportunity to improvise around the basic 4/4 timing. Practice for your next jam by playing sparingly. Vary your strums and capture the feel of the song. Try some fast down/up strums mixed with down and up strums, and even miss playing the strings altogether.

4/4

Intro
D⁷–D⁷–D⁷–D⁷, G

First verse
NO CHORD When you wake up in the C morning,
   Hear the ding-dong G ring,
You go marching to the D⁷ table,
   You see the same old G thing,
Knife and fork are on the C table,
   Ain't nothin' in my G pan,
If you say a thing D⁷ about it,
   You're in trouble with the G man.

Chorus
Let the midnight C special
   Shine a light on G me,
Let the midnight D⁷ special
   Shine its ever-loving light on G me.

Second verse
NO CHORD If you ever go to C Houston,
   Boy you'd better walk G right,
You better not D⁷ gamble,
   And you better not C fight,
Sheriff Benson will C arrest you,
   And he'll carry you G down,
And if the jury find you D⁷ guilty,
   You're penitentiary G bound.

Repeat Chorus

Third verse
NO CHORD Yonder comes Miss C Rosie,
   How the world do you G know?
I can tell her by her D⁷ apron
   And the dress that she G wore,
Umbrella on her C shoulder,
   Piece of paper in her G hand,
With a message for the D⁷ captain,
   Turn loose my G man.

Repeat Chorus

"SLOOP JOHN B" ▶ TRACK 14

Do nearly all the strumming with a relaxed forefinger and very little arm movement. A little practice will give you the sharp staccato sound that emphasizes the first beat of each bar and drives this song along. Once you have mastered the "groove," you can vary the strumming within the original arm movement. The strumming used in this song is more up strums than down. Listen for and copy the strum pattern: down, up/down/up, up/down. Try adding an occasional thumb pick on the G string. As well as playing one-note fingerpicking, you will need to pluck two or three strings together when you see them lined up in the tab. Note that the musical notation is included.

Go to *strummania.com.au* for audio/video.

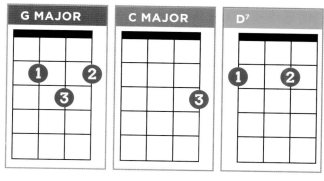

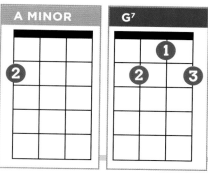

4/4

Intro
G–G–G–G, D⁷–D⁷–D⁷–D⁷, G–G–G–G

First verse
We **G** came on the sloop **C** John **G** B,
   My **G** grandfather **C** and **G** me,
Around Nassau town we did **D⁷** roam,
   Drinking all **G** night, **G⁷** we got into a **C** fight,
Am
Well, I **G** feel so broke up, **D⁷** I want to go **G** home.

Chorus
So **G** hoist up the John **C** B's **G** sails,
   See how the main- **C** sail **G** sets,
Call for the captain ashore and let me go **D⁷** home,
   Let me go **G** home **G⁷**,
I wanna go **C** home **Am**,
   Well, I **G** feel so broke up, **D⁷** I wanna go **G**
home.

Second verse
The **G** first mate he **C** got **G** drunk,
   And broke in the cap- **C** tain's **G** trunk,
Constable had to come and take him a- **D⁷** way,
   Sheriff John **G** Stone **G⁷**,
Why don't you leave me a- **C** lone **Am**,
   Well, I **G** feel so broke up, **D⁷** I wanna go **G**
home.

Repeat Chorus

Third verse
The **G** poor cook he got **C** the **G** fits,
   And threw away all **C** of my **G** grits,
And then he went and he ate up all of my **D⁷** corn,
   Let me go **G** home **G⁷**,
Why don't they let me go **C** home **Am**,
   This **G** is the worst trip **D⁷** I've ever been **G** on.

Repeat Chorus

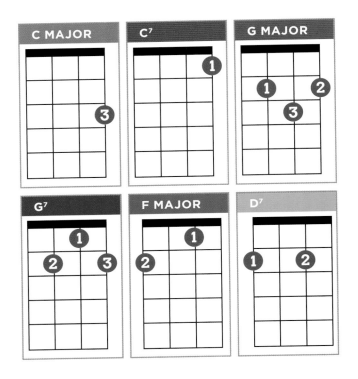

"UKULELE LADY"   ▶ TRACK 15

Think about moonlit beaches and swaying palms when you're playing this song.

4/4

Intro

The introduction for this song is a simple riff played on the A string. Strum twice on the third fret, twice on the second fret, twice on the open string, then twice on the second fret. Repeat.

Verse

If **C** you like Ukulele Lady, Ukulele Lady like-a you.

If **G⁷** you like to linger where it's shady, Ukulele Lady linger **C** too.

And **G⁷** she sees another Ukulele Lady fooling 'round with **C** you **C⁷**,

Repeat Twice

F Maybe she'll sigh,

C Maybe she'll cry,

D⁷ Maybe she'll find somebody else **G⁷** by and by.

To **C** sing to when it's cool and shady,

Where the tricky wicky wacky woo,

If **G⁷** you like Ukulele Lady, Ukulele Lady like-a **C** you.

(Sing the last line twice the second time through.)

"MY BLUE HEAVEN"

Lyrics by George Whiting, music by
Walter Donaldson, 1927

This is a laid-back song with lots of space in between the vocal lines, giving you the opportunity to experiment with your technique. If you are practicing a C scale, you can solo with the melody line or try some chord variations. You also have an opportunity to slide chords. For example, sliding the second position C chord means that you strike the chord shape on the second fret and, while it is ringing, slide up to the third fret.

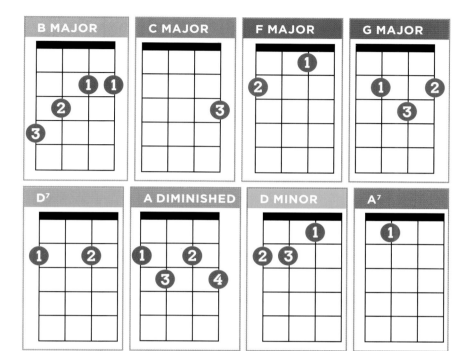

4/4

Intro

Strum the C major chord.

Slides

Here are the slides you'll use in this song. Play each one a few times until you get the hang of it, and then try playing along.

SLIDE #1 : Start by playing the B major chord shape on the third fret (C major). You will hold this chord shape throughout the slide. Strum on the third fret for three beats, slide to the second fret, strum once, and then slide back to the third fret and strum once.

SLIDE #2 : Play a B major chord shape on the third fret (C major) and hold this shape through the slide. Strum for three beats, slide to the second fret, strum once, slide to the first fret, and strum once. Finish the slide with an A7 chord.

Verse (repeat twice)

C When whippoorwills call **SLIDE #1** , and evening is nigh **SLIDE #2** ,

    I hurry to **D7** my **G7** blue **C** heaven.

C A turn to the right **SLIDE #1** , a little white light **SLIDE #2** , will lead you to

    D7 My **G7** blue **C** heaven.

A Dim You'll see a **F** smiling face,

    A7 A fireplace, a **Dm** cozy room **Dm7, Dm6** ,

G A little nest that's **G7** nestled where the **C** roses **A Dim** bloom **G7** .

    Just Mollie and **C** me **SLIDE #1** , and baby makes three **SLIDE #2** ,

We're happy in **D7** my **G7** blue **C** heaven.

Repeat the last line the second time you sing the verse.
Finish with a G chord shape on the 7th fret,
which is a C chord.

"CRAWDAD" ▶ TRACK 17

This song sounds good when accompanied by some easy plucking and light brushing of the strings. You can add emphasis to the start of each bar by slapping the G string with your thumb. You can also try plucking the outside strings together at the beginning of each bar that starts on a C chord. Try hammering on the G string as you play the F chord.

Turn the track volume down low and listen to what you are playing. This is a good song to learn how to jam with other people. See page 35 for the outro.

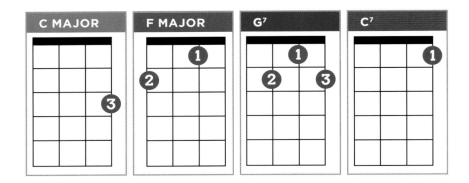

2/4

Intro
C–C–C-C, G⁷-G⁷-G⁷-G⁷, C–C–C–C

First verse
C You get a line and I'll get a pole, honey,
   You get a line and I'll get a pole **G⁷**, babe,
C You get a line and **C⁷** I'll get a pole
   And **F** we'll go down to that crawdad hole,
C Honey **G⁷**, sugar baby **C**, mine **F**, **C**.

Second verse
C Get up old man, you slept too late, honey,
   Get up old man, you slept too late **G⁷**, babe,
C Get up old man, you **C⁷** slept too late,
   F Last piece of crawdad's on your plate,
C Honey **G⁷**, sugar baby **C**, mine **F**, **C**.

Third verse
C Get up old woman, you slept too late, honey,

Get up old woman, you slept too late **G⁷**, babe,
C Get up old woman, you **C⁷** slept too late,
   F Crawdad man done passed our gate,
C Honey **G⁷**, sugar baby **C**, mine **F**, **C**.

Fourth verse
C Along came a man with a sack on his back, honey,
   Along came a man with a sack on his back **G⁷**,
   babe,
C Along came a man with a **C⁷** sack on his back,
   F Packin' all the crawdads he can pack,
C Honey **G⁷**, sugar baby **C**, mine **F**, **C**.

Fifth verse
C You get a line and I'll get a pole, honey,
   You get a line and I'll get a pole **G⁷**, babe,
C You get a line and **C⁷** I'll get a pole,
   And **F** we'll go down to the crawdad hole,
C Honey **G⁷**, sugar baby **C**, mine **F**, **C**.
C Honey **G⁷**, sugar baby **C**, mine **F**, **C**.

"HEY, GOOD LOOKIN'" ▶ TRACK 18

Words and music by Hank Williams

This classic is driven along by a solid beat that can easily be crushed by strummania. Keep the rhythm going and replace some full strums with single-string strums using your fingers and thumb. Now and again, try a hammer-on.

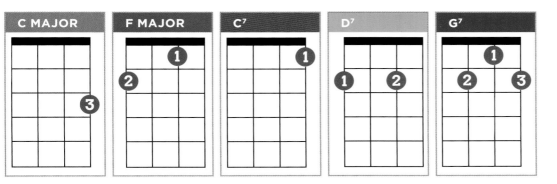

4/4

Intro
D⁷–D⁷–D⁷–D⁷, G⁷–G⁷–G⁷–G⁷, C–Rest–Rest–Rest

First verse
C Hey, good lookin', whatcha got cookin'?
    D⁷ How's about cookin' **G⁷** somethin' up with **C** me **G⁷**?
C Hey, sweet baby, don't you think maybe,
    D⁷ We could find us a **G⁷** brand new reci- **C** pe **C⁷**?
I got a **F** hot rod Ford and a **C** two dollar bill,
    F I know a spot right **C** over the hill,
F There's soda pop and the **C** dancin's free,
    So if you **D⁷** wanna have fun come a- **G⁷** long with me.

Chorus
C Hey, good lookin', whatcha got cookin'?
    D⁷ How's about cookin' **G⁷** somethin' up with **C** me?

Second verse
I'm **C** free and I'm ready so we can go steady,
    D⁷ How's about savin' **G⁷** all your time for **C** me?
C No more lookin', I know I've been tooken,
    D⁷ How's about keepin' **G⁷** steady **C** company **C⁷**?
I'm gonna **F** throw my date book **C** over the fence,
    And **F** find me one for **C** five or ten cents.
F Keep it 'til it's **C** covered with age,
    'Cause I'm **D⁷** writin' your name down on **G⁷** ev'ry page.

Final Chorus
C Hey, good lookin', whatcha got cookin'?
    D⁷ How's about cookin' **G⁷** somethin' up
D⁷ How's about cookin' **G⁷** somethin' up
    D⁷ How's about cookin' **G⁷** somethin' up with **C** me?

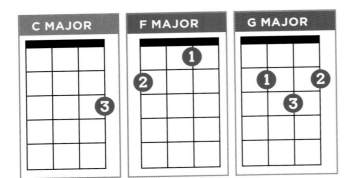

"AUSSIE BARBEQUE"

Words and music by Eric Bogle. Copyright Larrikin Publishing. Used with permission.

This is a fast strum played under the vocals. Here's some Aussie vocab you might not recognize:

aeroguard = insect repellent
mossies = insects
esky = beer cooler

dunny = toilet
snags = sausages

4/4

Intro
....
G–G–G–G, C–C–C–C

First verse
....
C When the summer sun shines brightly on **F** Australia's happy land,
   'Round **G** countless fires in strange attire you'll see many solemn **C** bands
Of glum Australians watching their **F** lunch go up in flames.
   By the **G** smoke and the smell you can plainly tell, its barbie time **C** again.

Chorus
....
C When the steaks are burning fiercely, when the **F** smoke gets in your eyes,
   When the **G** snags all taste of fried toothpaste,
And your mouth is full of **C** flies,
   It's a national institution,
It's **F** Australian through and through,
   So **G** come on mate, grab your plate,
Let's have a bar-b- **C** que!

Second verse
....
C The Scots eat lots of haggis, the **F** French eat snails and frogs,

The **G** Greeks go crackers over their moussaka, and the Chinese love hot- **C** dogs.
Welshmen love to have a leek, the **F** Irish love their stew,
   But you **G** just can't beat, the half cooked meat of an Aussie bar-b- **C** que!

Third verse
....
C There's flies stuck to the margarine, the **F** bread has gone rock hard,
   The **G** kids are fighting, the mossies are biting, who forgot the Aero- **C** guard?
There's bull ants in the Esky and the **F** beer is running out,
   And **G** what you saw in mum's coleslaw you just don't think **C** about.

Repeat Chorus

Fourth Verse
....
C And when the barbie's over and your **F** homeward way you wend,
   With a **G** queasy tummy on the family dunny, many lonely hours you **C** spend,
You might find yourself reflecting, as **F** many often do,
   Come **G** rain or shine that's the bloody last time You'll have a bar-b- **C** que!

Repeat Chorus

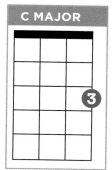
C MAJOR

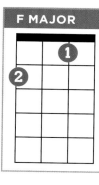
F MAJOR

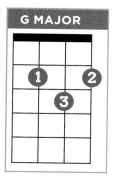
G MAJOR

"JAMAICA FAREWELL"

Lyrics and arrangement by Lord Burgess; first recorded version appeared on Harry Belafonte's 1956 album Calypso.

4/4

Intro

C–C–C-C, F–F–F-F, G–G–G–G, C–C–C–C

First verse

C Down the way, where the **F** nights are gay
And the sun **G** shines daily on the **C** mountaintop,
C I took a trip on a **F** sailing ship,
And when I **G** reached Jamaica, I **C** made a stop.

Chorus

But I'm **C** sad to say, I'm **F** on my way,
G Won't be back for **C** many a day,
My heart is down, my head is **F** turning around,
I had to **G** leave a little girl in **C** Kingston town.

Repeat chorus

Second verse

C Down at the market **F** you can hear
Ladies **G** cry out while on their **C** heads they bear
Ackee rice, salt **F** fish are nice,
And the **G** rum is fine any **C** time of year

Repeat chorus

Repeat chorus

Third verse

C Sounds of laughter **F** everywhere
And the **G** dancing girls sway **C** to and fro,
I must declare, my **F** heart is there,
'Though I've **G** been from Maine to **C** Mexico.

Repeat chorus

Repeat chorus

RESOURCES

CHORDS

Here's a handy guide to ukulele chords.

C MAJOR

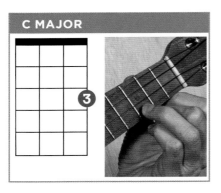

C MAJOR ON 3RD FRET

C MAJOR ON 7TH FRET

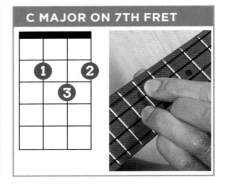

C BAR

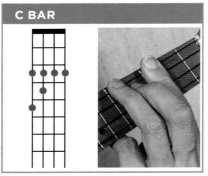

C⁷

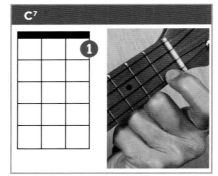

D MAJOR

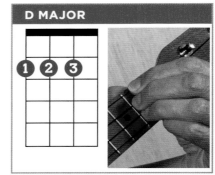

D BAR

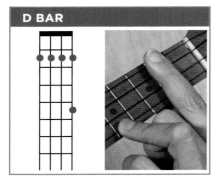

D MINOR

D⁷

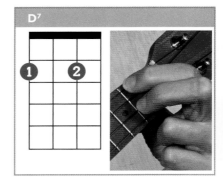

D⁷ BAR

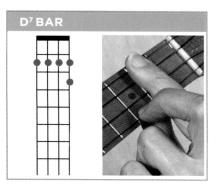

D MINOR 6

D MINOR 7

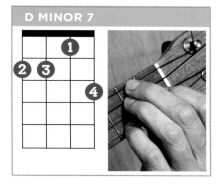

E MAJOR

E BAR

E⁷

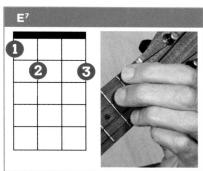

E⁷ BAR

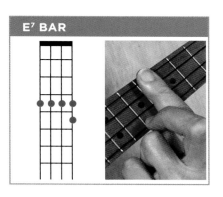

F MAJOR

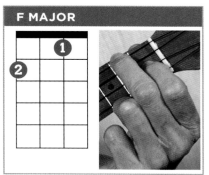

G MAJOR

G BAR
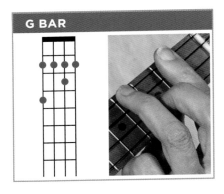

G⁷
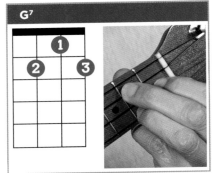

G⁷ BAR

A MAJOR

A BAR
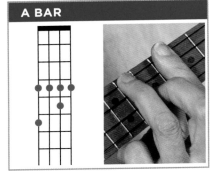

A⁷
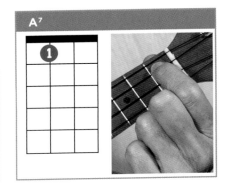

A⁷ BAR
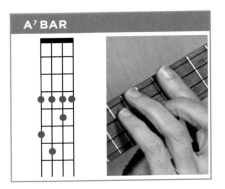

A MINOR
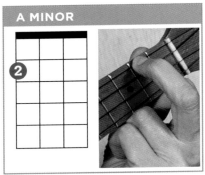

A DIMINISHED
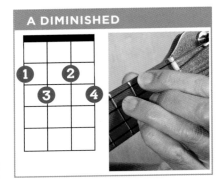

B MAJOR

B♭ MAJOR

Learn to Play the Ukulele Resources

THE UKE FESTIVAL CIRCUIT

Here is a listing of ukulele festivals worldwide, courtesy of Ukulele Hunt, *ukulelehunt.com*. Dates and times have a way of changing, and it has been known to rain . . . Always check online before you make any reservations.

BROWN COUNTY INN UKULELE FEST
Nashville, Indiana ....**January**
browncountyukefest.com

BLUE MUGS UKULELE FESTIVAL
New South Wales, Australia ....**February**
www.bluemugs.com.au

UKULELE PICNIC IN HAWAII
Honolulu ....**February**
www.ukulelepicnicinhawaii.org

UKULELE FESTIVAL HAWAII
Waikoloa ....**March**
www.ukulelefestivalhawaii.org

MELBOURNE UKULELE FESTIVAL
Melbourne, Australia ....**March**
www.muf.org.au

NORTHERN CALIFORNIA UKULELE FESTIVAL
Union City, California ....**April**
www.norcalukulelefestival.org

PLAY UKE FESTIVALS
Reno, Nevada ....**May**
www.playuke.net

UKULELE FESTIVAL OF SCOTLAND
Dumfries, Scotland ....**May**
ukulelefestivalofscotland.co.uk

UKULELE HOTSPOT WINTERSWIJK
Winterswijk, Netherlands......................May
www.profp.nl/hotspot/ww2018.html

AUSTRIAN UKULELE FESTIVAL
Graz, Austria ....May
https://www.ukulelefestival.at/

UKULELE WORLD CONGRESS
Needmore, Indiana..........................June
ukuleleworldcongress.wordpress.com

UKULELE FESTIVAL DORTMUND
Dortmund, Germany ....June

UKULELE FESTIVAL HAWAII
Waikiki..July
www.ukulelefestivalhawaii.org

UKULELE HOOLEY
Dublin, Ireland ....**August**
www.ukulelehooley.com

UKULELE FESTIVAL HAWAII
Maui .... September
www.ukulelefestivalhawaii.org

STRUMMIN' MAN
Panama City, Florida...........................October
www.standrewsukes.org

PLAY UKE FESTIVALS
Palm Springs, California ....October
www.playuke.net

WEST SOUND UKELELE FESTIVAL
Bremerton, Washington ....October
www.westsoundartandmusic.org

INTERNATIONAL UKULELE CEILIDH
Liverpool, Nova Scotia ....October
www.ukuleleceilidh.ca

BERLINER UKULELE FESTIVAL
Berlin, Germany ....October
berliner-ukulele-festival.de

NEWKULELE FESTIVAL
New Castle, Australia ....October
www.newkulelefestival.com

TAMPA BAY UKULELE GETAWAY (TBUG)
Tampa Bay, Florida ....November
www.tampabayukulele.com

UKULELE FESTIVAL HAWAII
Kauai..TBA
www.ukulelefestivalhawaii.org

UKEFEST VIRGINIA
Glen Allen, Virginia
www.ukefestva.com

HELPFUL SITES

Strummania

Visit our very own *strummania.com.au* for all things ukulele. Note: We also sell ukuleles; inquire through our site's contact page.

Dr. Uke

This site—*www.doctoruke.com*—has song sheets and MIDI tracks that you can play along with.

The Fabulous Songbook

Though it is no longer updated, at *kristinhall.org* you'll find the words and chord progressions to just about every song you'll ever need to know.

Humble Uker Ramblings

The site *humbleuker.blogspot.com* is full of links to songs and other uke websites.

New York Ukulele School

Founded by Mark Michaels, *www.newyorkukuleleschool.com* offers lessons in all styles of uke playing and has mp3 and video clips.

Richard Gillmann's Free Ukulele Tab Links

At *nwfolk.com/uketabs.html* you can find heaps of ukulele websites for songs, sheet music, and more.

Taunton Ukulele Strummers

For a link to songbooks you can print for free, check out *www.tusc.co.uk*.

Ukulele Hunt

Here, at one of the most comprehensive sites dedicated to the uke, you'll find a list of festivals and tons of other great stuff: *ukulelehunt.com*.

Ukulele Boogaloo

The site *www.alligatorboogaloo.com/uke* includes links to organizations and clubs, performers' websites, instructional information, songbooks, and ukulele makers and retailers.

Ukulele Underground

This well-designed site includes forums for beginners, contests, regional get-togethers, and more: *www.ukuleleunderground.com*.

BUY A (REALLY NICE) UKE

Peter Hurney, California
www.pohakuukulele.com

Jay Lichty, North Carolina
ichtyguitars.com

Chuck Moore, Hawaii
www.moorebettahukes.com

Mya-Moe Ukuleles, Washington
www.myamoeukuleles.com

Palm Tree Ukuleles, Colorado
palmtreeukuleles.com

Gary Zimnicki, Michigan
www.zimnicki.com

INDEX

More Great Books
from Fox Chapel Publishing

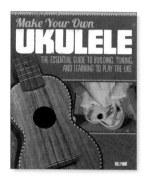

Make Your Own Ukulele
The Essential Guide to Building, Tuning, and Learning to Play the Uke
BILL PLANT
Paperback • 96 pages • 8.5" x 11"
978-1-56523-565-6 • #5656 • $17.95

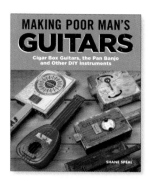

Making Poor Man's Guitars
Cigar Box Guitars, the Frying Pan Banjo, and Other DIY Instruments
SHANE SPEAL
Paperback • 176 pages • 8" x 10"
978-1-56523-946-3 • #9463 • $19.99

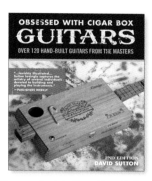

Obsessed with Cigar Box Guitars
Over 120 Hand-Built Guitars from the Masters
DAVID SUTTON
Paperback • 208 pages • 7" x 9"
978-1-62008-313-0 • #3130 • $19.99

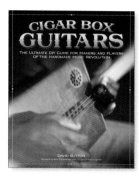

Cigar Box Guitars
The Ultimate DIY Guide for the Makers and Players of the Handmade Music Revolution
DAVID SUTTON
Paperback • 224 pages • 8.5" x 11"
978-1-56523-547-2 • #5472 • $29.95

Handmade Music Factory
The Ultimate Guide to Making Foot-Stompin Good Instruments
MIKE ORR
Paperback • 160 pages • 8.5" x 11"
978-1-56523-559-5 • #5595 • $22.95

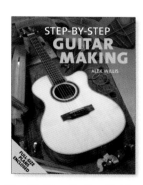

Step By Step Guitar Making
Full-Size Plans Enclosed
ALEX WILLIS
Paperback • 144 pages • 8.25" x 11"
978-1-56523-331-7 • #3317 • $22.95

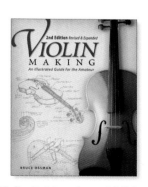

Violin Making, Second Edition Revised and Expanded
An Illustrated Guide for the Amateur
BRUCE OSSMAN
Paperback • 104 pages • 8.5" x 11"
978-1-56523-435-2 • #4352 • $19.95

Custom Wooden Music Boxes for the Scroll Saw
Over 45 Projects from the Berry Basket Collection
RICK AND KAREN LONGABAUGH
Paperback • 192 pages • 8.5" x 11"
978-1-56523-301-0 • #3018 • $19.95

Look For These Books At Your Favorite Retailer
or call 800-457-9112 • visit FoxChapelPublishing.com

ABOUT THE AUTHORS

We both came from musical families at a time when family and visitors sang around the piano, before TV. In the 1960s and 1970s, popular American music hit our airwaves and fostered our interest in the guitar. Traditional Australian music re-emerged in the 1970s, and people took to playing guitar, mandolin, harmonica, fiddle, button accordion, and percussion. Before we met, we played guitar in bush bands at dances, which in those days were held in town halls, shearing sheds, and even outside.

Our love affair with the ukulele started during a record-breaking heat wave. Since our house had only one air-conditioned room and Trisha was feeling the heat, she shut herself in to learn the ukulele. Days passed and she finally emerged a dedicated, but rough, ukulele player. Bill said "wow," bought a ukulele, and joined in. The ukulele has since become our favorite instrument: it is portable, versatile, and fun.

Having had some experience with community music, and being the only ukulele players in town, we were asked to establish a community ukulele band. To everyone's surprise, 60 people signed up for the first series of classes, followed by another 50 in the next class. There followed a crazy series of 10 weekly lessons culminating in a gala performance in the local town hall. Since then we have taught over 1,500 people to play at schools, workshops, and festivals all over the country. Our ukuleles are a constant travel companion; we carry them in a soft gig bag that is easily slung over a shoulder and passes as hand luggage on aircraft. In addition to offering group workshops, we also give ukulele lessons via Skype, as well as make custom ukuleles (and mandolins and cigar box guitars) for sale—address inquiries to billplant23@gmail.com if you're interested.

www.strummania.com.au

TRACKLIST FOR THE CD

TRACKS FOR PRACTICE

1: Tuning Reference
2: Frère Jacques
3: Strumming Patterns
4: Strumming in ¾ Time
5: Picking Practice
6: Scale Practice
7: Playing by Ear
8: Learn to Play the Ukulele Overnight Blues

SONGS TO PLAY

9: Polly Wolly Doodle
10: Pay Me My Money Down
11: Jambalaya
12: This Train Is Bound for Glory
13: Midnight Special
14: Sloop John B
15: Ukulele Lady
16: My Blue Heaven
17: Crawdad
18: Hey, Good Lookin'
19: Aussie BBQ